In the Name of the Goddess

Environment and Religion in Feminist-Womanist, Queer, and Indigenous Perspectives

Series Editor: Gabrie'l Atchison

Environment and Religion in Feminist-Womanist, Queer, and Indigenous Perspectives is a series that explores the subject of ecofeminism from feminist-womanist, queer, and indigenous perspectives. The governing assumption of the series is that ecofeminism is not only a mode of scholarly discourse and analysis but also a hub for social formation and action. What distinguishes this series in particular is that it focuses on ecofeminism as a disciplinary matrix through which the voices of women, particularly women of color, and indigenous peoples can speak from their religious and spiritual traditions and practices to address the environmental challenges and concerns of the age. Volumes in this series will attend to the environmental and ecological issues that impact women, people of color, and indigenous populations, as these communities are, in almost all respects, the most immediately threatened by contemporary climate and ecological changes and catastrophes. Works in the series will focus on the history; scholarly resources and perspectives; constructive practices; religious, spiritual, and natural traditions from which these voices speak; and how these can provide alternative narratives, illuminate hidden agendas, and generate resistance to environmental and religious racism and exploitation.

Titles in the series

Mapping Gendered Ecologies: Engaging with and beyond Ecowomanism and Ecofeminism, edited by K. Melchor Quick Hall and Gwyn Kirk
In the Name of the Goddess: A Biophilic Ethic, by Donna Giancola

In the Name of the Goddess

A Biophilic Ethic

Donna Giancola

LEXINGTON BOOKS
Lanham • Boulder • New York • London

Published by Lexington Books
An imprint of The Rowman & Littlefield Publishing Group, Inc.
4501 Forbes Boulevard, Suite 200, Lanham, Maryland 20706
www.rowman.com

6 Tinworth Street, London SE11 5AL, United Kingdom

British Library Cataloguing in Publication Information Available

Library of Congress Cataloging-in-Publication Data Available

ISBN 978-1-7936-0154-4 (cloth : alk. paper)
ISBN 978-1-7936-0156-8 (pbk. : alk. paper)
ISBN 978-1-7936-0155-1 (electronic)

♾™ The paper used in this publication meets the minimum requirements of American
National Standard for Information Sciences—Permanence of Paper for Printed Library
Materials, ANSI/NISO Z39.48-1992.

This is for Magick . . . In all innocence!

Contents

Acknowledgments

With great respect and love, I begin by thanking all our mothers and fore-mothers everywhere. Specifically, I thank my own mother for teaching me, Mary Esther for guiding me, Mary Daly for not so gently putting me back on the path, and Maureen for being "there."

For those on this side, I would like to thank my beloved friend and colleague, Dr. Wanda Torres Gregory, for her unflinching care and generosity of mind and heart. Also, I would like to thank my dear friend, neighbor, and life administrator, Barbara Coffey, for her constant encouragement and for always propping me back up. And finally, I would like to thank Suffolk University for their support, especially my chair, Dr. Evgenia Cherkasova.

Introduction

In the Name of the Goddess

In the Name of the Goddess evolved quite naturally into a biophilic ethic. I initially intended to write about the invocation and evocation of the Goddess. Specifically, I wanted to explore the energetic meaning(s) of calling forth the powers, myths, and symbols of the Great-Mother Goddess(es) to see what they could do for us today in terms of ethical practices and eco-justice. But first, steps needed to be taken to unearth and unfold the primal roots and elemental relationship of justice and being in the Goddess traditions. The last sentence of this book is where I would have liked to have begun.

By definition, *biophilia* means the love of life. A biophilic ethic centers on concerns for the earth, environmental sustainability, and social justice. Ecofeminists and environmental activists from around the world are engaged in moral and political debates about the ecological well-being and fate of our planet. However, while the awareness of the problems facing us is at an all-time high, there are many faults in the tools, methods, and thinking used to combat our global problems. Religious, political, and cultural practices serve as impediments to change. Because social domination is not different from the domination of nature, a biophilic ethic must and can provide an organic, holistic, and inclusive approach for sorting and creating policies and practices that reflect the interconnections and interrelations of nature and all life on this planet. This work puts the locus of biophilia in the ecofeminist and environmental movements. My intention is to expand on the meaning of this term, "biophilia," and lay the foundation for a radical ecofeminist ethics. Going beyond traditional androcentric ethical theories, biophilia heartens a dynamic holistic ethics of interconnectedness, ecological sustainability, and ecojustice. I used the term "biophilia," here not as a principle of ethics, or as an "ought" but rather as an immediate/unmediated energetic response to all life, to other

1

humans, to other species, to the natural world. As living creatures with hearts and minds, we are naturally predisposed to love life. This predisposition is the birth of compassion and the emergence of biophilia.

Biophilia has its historical roots in the ancient goddess traditions[1] and has recently seen a resurgence in such fields as biology, technology, design, environmental studies, and ecofeminism. Edward Wilson in his book *Biophilia* asks: "Is it possible that humanity will love life enough to save it?"[2] As a naturalist and scientist Wilson defines biophilia from a biological perspective as "an innate tendency to focus on life and lifelike processes."[3] Wilson goes on to argue that we are biologically and mentally invested not just in our own survival but also in the survival of other species. Biophilia is a biological fact and is hardwired into the human brain. Wilson further maintains that because of recent advances in biology we have a new way of seeing human relationships with the natural world that "is congenial to the inner direction of biophilia." In this rare sense, "instinct is aligned with reason."[4] Wilson calls for a conservation ethic based on biophilia, claiming that "the future of the conservation movement depends on such advances in moral reasoning."[5] Admittedly, however, he does not develop it himself.

After establishing a biological basis for biophilia, Wilson focuses more on sociobiology rather than developing what he means by "biophilia." Since then, biophilia has gained some popularity among other scientists for how it can inform our affiliations to other species. Also, and interestingly, biophilia has even made its way into architectural design including everything from homes and apartments to office spaces. It seems people like and appreciate nature and are happier when surrounded by living things. Hence, the cross cultural design practices of incorporating the outdoors with the inside of our homes. But biophilia is more than a warm fuzzy feeling or an aesthetics. It is a universal experience, among and across all species. It has not only a biological basis but also a rational one as well. Reason tells us that we cannot live apart from the other species or the natural world and expect to survive. Reason dictates that we learn to live well with ourselves, with others, and with nature. Biophilia offers an inclusive and expansive vision of an ethics rooted not in abstract principle but in the core of our being and the recess of our psyche. In the face of our concurrent global problems of pandemics, oppression, pollution, and poverty of body, mind, and spirit, biophilia is a natural and primordial life-affirming response.

In his chapter "Malignant Aggression: Necrophilia," from *The Anatomy of Human Destructiveness*, Erich Fromm in his discussion of Freud's life and death instincts, designates only a paragraph or two on biophilia. He states that in comparing the death (*thanatos*) and life instincts (*eros*) "biophilia is the passionate love of life and all that is alive, it is the wish for further growth."[6] The biophilious person, as Fromm calls them, "sees the whole rather than only the parts, structures rather than summations," choosing "love, reason and example rather than force or cutting things apart, by the bureaucratic manner of administering people as if they were things."[7]

He contends, and rightly so, that a biophilic ethic has its own set of principles, where good is what serves and enhances life and growth, and evil is what stifles life and serves death and destruction.[8] However, Fromm says little else specifically about biophilia or what would be the basis for a biophilic ethic.

Taking all of life into account, its elemental and evolutionary processes, the environment, and social and ecological changes spanning hundreds of thousands of years pushes the parameters of human consciousness into an expanded ethical awareness. However, traditional ethical theories because of their patriarchal and anthropomorphic perspectives are ill-equipped to rise to this challenge of seeing beyond. As an alternative voice, Mary Daly, a leading feminist and ecofeminist thinker, states in her feminist manifesto:

> I am now declaring that the intentions, motives and views of Radical Elemental Feminist are focused on one central cause: the expansion of *Biophilia*, which means "the Original Lust for Life that is at the core of all Elemental E-motion."[9]

Daly goes on to comment on that the fact that "necrophilia" is in the dictionary and "biophilia" is and of itself significant. "It is related to the absence of love of life from the patriarchal world."[10] Unfortunately, Daly herself does not go on to develop a biophilic ethic either.

By the very title of this book, *In the Name of the Goddess*, I am affirming the source of biophilia as the principle of creation in the Great-Mother Goddess, for She holds the mystery of love. My overarching thesis is that a biophilic ethic emerges as the just actualization and radicalization of love. But here is the problem: like the majority of us, I am no expert on love, and I am no fan of Plato either. His elitist philosophy was a prime force in further eclipsing the primordial oneness of the ancient Goddess traditions. But, still, he wrote some beautiful dialogues. Not the least of which was the *Symposium*. The *Symposium* is a classical reference on love, and here, Plato lets a few secrets slip. Notably, the *Symposium* is one of the few dialogues in which Socrates puts forth an actual philosophical position as opposed to a philosophical method, but more importantly, it is the only dialogue where Socrates defers to someone else's teachings, namely, that of his teacher, Diotima's. The fact that Plato espouses the ancient Goddess teachings as coming forth from a woman/priestess, is no subtle point. What the Mysteries reveal about the origins, function, nature, and truth of love could only come forth from a Goddess. It is a philosophy of love based on the roots and recesses of life.

According to an ancient Greek myth, Eros, the Greek god of love, was conceived on the night of Aphrodite's (the Greek Goddess of Love) birthday party. Eros is the offspring of an unlikely duo. His father is Poverty and his mother is Plenty. Conceived by Necessity and Resourcefulness, love is never full, but never completely lacking either. Abundance, like love, is not about wanting and having, but balance and flow, back and forth, like the ebbing and flowing of the tide. Emptiness and fullness and emptiness and fullness, we have, and, we have not. To invoke abundance into our lives (in its many forms), we must embody its essence and hold ourselves against the sway of changing tides, knowing that true abundance is in the flow itself.

As Socrates tells the story of Diotima's teachings on the mythical origins of love, we are reminded of its dialectical nature as the child of plenty and poverty, abundance and emptiness. Further, we are reminded through Socrates that love is neither young nor old, beautiful nor ugly, mortal nor immortal, but somewhere in between; an intermediate spirit that carries human hearts and hopes from earth to heaven, and messages from the gods/goddesses to humans. According to Socrates, Diotima, referring to the Mystery traditions of ancient goddess worship, instructs him in the "lesser Mysteries." She also reluctantly attempts to initiate Socrates into the higher teachings, and here we move beyond mere philosophy.

In approaching the *Symposium*, emphasis is usually placed on the function of love as an ascent from the particular to the principle, from love of a body to love of knowledge, and to love of the pure form of beauty. Diotima instructs Socrates as follows:

> And the true order of going, or being led by another, to things of love is to begin from the beauties of the earth and mount upward for the sake of that other beauty, using these steps only, and from one going to two, and from two to all fair forms, and from fair forms to fair practices, and from fair practices to fair notions, until from fair he arrives at the notion of absolute beauty, and at last knows what the essence of beauty is.[11]

This accent of love demonstrates that love is ultimately love of the good. Thus, *eros* (romantic love) becomes *philia* (universal love). In moving beyond the particulars to the pure form, we learn that love is not bound by images or conditions but by truth. This is more or less the traditional interpretation of Plato's *Symposium*, complete with his abstract hyperrationalistic views and disembodied forms. However, there is a deeper meaning still, albeit not one recognized by mainstream philosophy or philosophers.

The nature of love does not arise out of Socrates's speech, but from what Diotima leaves unspoken for others to see: that the nature of love is not contained by the *logos*, it cannot be spoken, in keeping with the higher

Mysteries; it can only be revealed.[12] Our ascending journey to the truth of love takes away all the conditions until love in its pure form is revealed as unconditioned, disclosing its essential nature as emptiness, and therein lies its power as unbounded. Because of emptiness something new gets born. This is why the most obvious point about the truth of love must be revealed by a woman, out of the womb of emptiness comes creativity, generation, production, and reproduction.[13] It is revelatory and necessarily born from the womb. Emptiness is the womb for the birth of vision, and maybe it is a new vision of love that we all need right now, from *eros* to *agape,* and perhaps, we can skip over that pesky "love of wisdom" and go right to biophilia?

In constructing a biophilic ethic, it is not my intention simply to propagate feminist or ecofeminist theories, but rather to utilize them and ground them in their historical origins in ancient myth and philosophical principles. *In the Name of the Goddess* is an ecofeminist ethic, to be sure, as it entails the parallels between the domination of women and the domination of nature by patriarchy. By beginning with the goddess, the title of this work gives notice that like some ecofeminist philosophy this work has a nature-based spiritual component. As a biophilic ethic, it reflects on humanity's shared experience with and within the natural world and seeks unifying principles that respect our commonalities as well as our differences. There is always a danger of universalism in constructing an ethics, and this is especially true for ecofeminists. Some ecofeminist thinkers are critical of essentialism for relying too heavily on women's relationship to the natural world, and thereby reinforcing oppressive patriarchal stereotypes, divisions, and norms. But both women and men, in addition to being biologically conditioned, have been socially, culturally and psychological constrained by too many "isms" and dualities. Gender is a prime example. While the biological is the anatomical, gender identity, and sexual orientation are on a continuum, and are nonbinary.

One of the central and defining pillars of *In the Name of the Goddess* is the radical assumption of the nondual nature of reality. The majority of arguments and counterarguments of feminists and ecofeminists stop at the surface and do not lay bare the uncritical assumption of dualism itself. It is insufficient to deconstruct the master narrative from within. Nondual thinking is the liberating force for recognizing the impartiality of the wholeness of reality.[14] Note: I invoke the Goddess, not as a genuine ontological opposition to patriarchal concepts, but as a deeper ground for dispensing with duality all together. The image/metaphor of the goddess is meant to be symbolic of the continuum of an all-encompassing reality, and is used as a counterbalancing measure against all dualistic distinctions, isms, schisms, and constructions. Nondual thinking does not stand in opposition to duality, but instead embraces it. And, as I will be discussing later, reality itself, is, nonbinary, not dual, "not two/not one, not separate, not apart."[15]

Beginning with a cross-cultural (Asian and European) comparative analysis of ancient goddess traditions, the first chapter focuses on the philosophical and historical emergence of our earliest conceptions of justice as a living connection portraying a cosmological and ecological balance. Comparing and contrasting the ancient worldview to our modern-day patriarchal systems of domination, the next chapter highlights such problems as globalization, food, land, ecological destruction, and loss of biodiversity. The subsequent chapters will discuss how the ecofeminist principles of embodiment, interconnection, ecojustice, and sustainability form a liberating alternative to traditional ethical theories and oppressive practices. I will argue that the ecofeminist response alone is not sufficient without a return to our philosophical roots in myth and ancient nature-based beliefs and practices.[16] This will culminate in the construction of a biophilic ethic that enables us to end some of the schisms produced by planetary oppression and promote an earth- and life-centered consciousness. The final section will propose an infusion of ethical and spiritual practices that help frame a conscious evolution toward personal and planetary healing. Most importantly, this section will attempt to give voice to alternative ways of knowing, responding, and participating in the creation of a global justice.

Throughout this project, I propose to confront the destructive nature of patriarchy and ask whether the principles of an ecofeminist/biophilic ethic can reveal a path beyond dualistic distinctions in politics, culture, and nature. In the end, my motivating question is can a biophilic ethic provide an integrated perspective for cosmological justice and right relations in a global community? I take my cues from nature, and from those who have stood on the precipice of a new horizon of thought. The evolution of human consciousness will eventually move beyond patriarchal modalities and thought-forms into a life-affirming vision. The human spirit will not allow itself to be held captive indefinitely. The inspiration for and purpose of human life is not to be comfortable but to evolve.

Admittedly, there are many who would deny the presence of the Great-Mother Goddess: Her story, Her role in creation, being, immanence and transcendence, and Her very existence. Some of the disputes concerning Her presence and the emergence of ancient matriarchal societies in general are still disputed. Some disputes are theological, some historical and academic.[17] Most are politically charged. After all, what would it mean if we envisioned the Divine as feminine? Imagine a political structure based on the principles of life, interconnection, inclusion, equality, and cooperation. I worship the Goddess because I believe in life, and because I want to live in a world where everyone gets to eat. To be in touch with the Goddess is to be attuned to the forces of nature, the cycles of life, seeing the sway of all things in a higher order where compassion and oneness are the ground at our feet. When we put ourselves in tune with the ancient teachings and ways of the Goddess a new vision arises eclipsing into a landscape for spiritual consciousness that focuses on nature and life's energies.

The earth is alive. This is not a new idea; it comes to us from archaic myth and philosophy. Although it was not until recently that science confirmed the ancient Greek myth of the goddess, Gaia, that the theory gained some acceptance. James Lovelock, a chemist, put forth in the 1970s the "Gaia Hypothesis," claiming that the earth was a living organism. He maintained that our living planet functioned as its own self-sustaining ecosystem where the earth and its life forms coevolve to promote planetary well-being and balance.[18] Seeing the earth as a living interconnected whole changes the perspective by forcing us to confront the theoretical and practical implications of the infinite threads of interconnections that is life itself. The acknowledgment and appreciation for the earth, nature's processes, and interconnectedness that are woven into the myths of the ancients are foundational to a biophilic ethic and transcend the conflicting and waring perspectives that dominate our modern, predominantly western, mechanical perspective of industrial "progress." But the mythical roots merely preserve a glimpse of what has been degraded through the modernization process, the paternalization, segregation, and compartmentalization of the material realm, and parallel codification of customs, mores, and practices.

Fundamental to the shift away from humanity's sense of interconnectedness to nature was the subordination of women specifically because of their prior revered mythical status of inherently being and representing a connection with nature and the cyclical life cycle of living beings. The religious philosophical effect was a shift from pantheistic nature worship to patriarchal theism, which is evidenced in the religious, social, economic, and political structures of localities and nations around the world, resulting in a self-destructive imbalance that radiates through our modern paradigms and into all of our lives.

While it may seem easy to dismiss the harsher realities of our postmodern global destruction of the environment, people, and animals as distant and other, or abstract and removed, the interconnectedness principle lying dormant in the echoes of our archaic myths attests that this is more than mere myth. We are in fact interconnected with, and codependent upon the survival and success of all peoples and beings living on this planet. Their survival is our survival. We are also dependent upon the health of our planet. One who appreciates interconnection and the sacredness of women and nature has a different understanding of the value and purpose of life. While the earth and humans are capable of adaptation, the fact that world leaders and mainstream society are avoiding critical discourse and still debating about the issue of sustainability only further proves that our appreciation for the sacredness of nature has been lost, or severely crippled, and we must build some momentum to slowly turn the tides. Women's energies can create a new world based on a biophilic ethic and a return to a living justice. We can speed up the remediation/healing if we consider the reflexive role of myth in creating a new totemic.

A biophilic ethic based on the principles of the Goddess traditions requires both a metaphysical and an epistemological paradigmatic shift because the reality of the whole exceeds the dimensions of a very limited and divisive patriarchal worldview. The goddess metaphor is necessary for us to break out of the rule of the "king." It is not by replacing one sovereign with another but by naming the Goddess as such that we can empower ourselves to identify with that which is life-affirming. When we throw off the yoke of patriarchy, we discover infinite possibilities that previously we did not know existed because we were unable to see beyond the perspective of duality and the tyranny of the "fathers." It is time for us to remove the gods from their pedestals, and for that you need a Goddess. Naming the Goddess is an all-encompassing act of liberation and pronouncement for ourselves, all living beings and the planet. Her ways can teach us that the path to a compassionate ethics is a path that as humans requires us to cultivate a broader and holistic perspective in the context of the All. The Goddess teaches us to embrace the totality of reality. She is matter and energy, accessible, transcendent, immanent, intimate, and worldly. It is time to return to the Earth. Welcome Home!

NOTES

1. Marija Gimbutas, *The Language of the Goddess* (San Francisco: Harper and Row, 1989), xix–xx. "The main theme of the Goddess symbolism is the mystery of birth and death and the renewal of life, not just human but all life on earth and indeed in the whole cosmos. Symbols and images cluster around the parthenogenetic (self-generating) Goddess and her basic function as the Giver of Life, Wielder of Death, and not less importantly as Rengeratrix."

2. Edward O. Wilson, *Biophilia* (Cambridge, MA; London, England: Harvard University Press, 1984), 145.

3. Ibid., 1.

4. Ibid., 2.

5. Ibid., 119.

6. Erich Fromm, *The Anatomy of Human Destructiveness* (New York; Chicago; San Francisco: Holt, Rinehart and Winston, 1973), 365.

7. Ibid.

8. Ibid., 366.

9. Mary Daly, *Quintessence . . . Realizing the Archaic Future* (Boston: Beacon Press, 1998), 7. Daly goes on to say that "Pure Lust is the Nemesis of patriarchy, the necrophilic state."

10. Ibid., 7–8.

11. Plato, *Symposium*, trans. Benjamin Jowett (Indianapolis: The Library of Liberal Arts, The Bob Merrill Company Inc., 1976), 52 (210c–212a).

12. In speaking of the Mystery Traditions, I am specifically referring to the teaching of the Eleusinian Mysteries which were practiced in ancient Greece on top of Mt. Eleusis.

13. Tsultrim Allione, *Women of Wisdom* (London, Arkana, 1986), 23: "The essential emptiness is the primary matrix of existence and is therefore called 'The Mother of Creation.' It is the basic space that permeates everything and undermines the ego. Voidness is the expression of space. The Great-Mother principle is the space that gives birth to the phenomenal world."

14. Jennifer Crawford, *Spiritually Engaged Knowledge* (Hampshire, England: Ashgate, 2005), 91. "I argue that the nondual approach, precisely by tackling dualism *per se*, may be just what is needed in the contemporary situation where multiple forms of oppression operate systemically across the boundaries of multiple dualism."

15. Rick Fields, "The Very Short Sutra on the Meeting of the Buddha and the Goddess," *Dharma Gaia*, ed. Alan Hunt Badiner (Berkeley, CA: Parallax Press, 1990), 7.

16. Rosemary Radford Ruether, *Integrating Ecofeminism Globalization and World Religions* (New York: Roman and Littlefield Publishers, Inc., 2005), 93. According to Ruether: "Women need to claim this affinity with nature and take the lead in creating an new earth-based spirituality and practice of care for the earth."

17. Walter Burkert, *Greek Religion*, trans. John Raffan (Cambridge, MA: Harvard University Press, 1989), 351 n. 22. Burkert takes issues with the nature and mythical origins of matriarchal societies claiming that "Matriarchy in its true sense has not been shown to have existed anywhere in the Aegean or Near Eastern prehistory."

18. www.nytimes.com 1989/08/29>science-evolving-theory-earth.

Chapter 1

Radical Matriarchy

The Story of the Goddess

I use the term "radical" here in its initial meaning as "root." This chapter establishes how the principles of the ancient matriarchal traditions lay the groundwork for the emergence of a biophilic ethic. Tracing back to the origins and prehistory of ancient goddess worship in the philosophical traditions of ancient Greece and India will reveal the primordial life-affirming principles of cosmic order and justice embodied in the matriarchal worldview. These both predate and differ from patriarchy. This chapter will demonstrate that the role of justice in both traditions is higher than law, higher even than the gods, and creates a fragile balance between human and cosmological order.

In the beginning was the Goddess, more precisely, before the beginning was the Goddess. She was there before history was even created. Goddess worship was our ancient ancestors' earliest means of understanding the genesis of the universe and cosmic order. The Great Mother Goddess was worshipped all over the world for the first 25,000 years of human life on this planet. From Greece to India to Babylon to Sumer to Africa, she is the Goddess of a thousand names. From tribal to cosmic, she emerged as the primary deity of human consciousness. Yet, her story is seldom told and even more seldomly taken seriously.

Yet, what does it mean to worship the Goddess? It means a fundamental recognition that the Earth, the Universe is alive: creation, motion, change, transformation, vibration, harmony, and balance—these are the characteristics of all life. To be in touch with the Goddess is to be attuned with the forces of Nature, the cycles of life, seeing the sway of all things in a higher order, where compassion and oneness are the ground at our feet. Her truths are alive, buried in the myths of tradition and history. Her revelations speak to our primal connections to the earth, to the plants, to animals, to each other, and to the matrix of life itself. The goddess myth of life, death, and rebirth is reproduced in all major world religions. Looking beyond the man-made facade of patriarchal traditions is to see from the eyes of the Goddess and recognize the sacredness of life.

The Great Mother Goddess of the ancient world as the source of life and creative energy is primordial oneness. However, this is not the oneness of a static and transcendent anthropomorphic being who stands apart from "his" creation, but rather the undifferentiated wholeness of the primal pulsations that give rise to being and nonbeing, to the nonduality of what is. As this chapter will reveal, the integrity of the Goddess as the original source of life becomes eclipsed, quite intentionally, with the advent of philosophy and superimposed rationalistic conceptions. Prior to patriarchal dualistic distinctions of mind and matter, being and nonbeing, light and dark, the Goddess manifested all things, and all beings were said to have their life in Her. Understanding the nonduality of the Great Mother Goddess provides the ground for a biophilic ethic. But whence she did she emerge, where has she gone and how do we return to her roots?

The prehistory of the Great Mother Goddess does not come to us from our history books or traditional philosophy or world religions. For the last two thousand years, she has hardly been mentioned since patriarchal monotheistic religions have taken over. In fact, the existence of matriarchal societies and cultures has been called into question by male scholars from across the disciplines.[1] It is not until the early to mid-twentieth century that she makes a reappearance to us, as female archaeologists begin to reexamine and reinterpret what their male counterparts had assumed were mere "transitional objects." From all over the world, goddess sculptures were found, some dating back to 24,000 BCE. The most famous of these today is the Venus of Willendorf with her abundant curves and powerful body connecting the power of women to the power of the earth. These figurines of the Goddess come in various shapes and sizes, separated by geography and culture; nevertheless, they share striking similarities. Most of these artifacts date back to the Paleolithic and Neolithic periods and represent a cannon of beliefs and universally held principles of ancient goddess worshipping societies.[2]

The stories differ from culture to culture, but the meaning of the myth stays the same. Myth is a vehicle of transformation from the everyday secular consciousness to a primordial awareness of eternal models of the spiritual journey. Myth always unveils a deep mystery.[3] Myth is never just myth. To embody the goddess myth is a revolution of consciousness. All major world religious traditions have goddess myth at their core. Life, death rebirth, the cycles of nature, the modes of consciousness, the unending revolutions of creation, the turning of the wheel, what is manifest and what is unmanifest; this is the dance of life.

Prior to the onset of patriarchy, women were at the center. They were the healers, the shamans, the prophetesses, the high priestesses, and the goddesses. Throughout Greece, the mystery cults of Demeter, Aphrodite, and Athena were all enacted according to the same themes. In Eleusis, for example, which is the only place where the mysteries of Demeter were re-enacted, initiation was confirmed through the power of the goddess herself. Demeter, the Corn Goddess, Earth Mother, challenges the god of death, Hades, to return her daughter, Persephone, to her from the underworld, or else Demeter will withhold her life-giving energies from the earth and nothing may grow. In India, where myth is still taken seriously, there is the dance of the god Shiva on the wheel of life, where the goddesses *Maya, Shakti,* and *Deva* help form the Hindu pantheon of gods and goddesses representing the two aspects of creation. In India, the Goddess Shakti is highly regarded as vital energy of life, the charge to existence, the unseen force that gives rise to the universe. In some yoga practices in India, the feminine was seen as transformative creative energy, simultaneously expressing the emptiness and the fullness of what is. In Tibet, the reverence for the creative powers of women has its origins in the shamanic tradition of the ancient Bon civilization. In ancient Babylon, Innana descends into the underworld to save her lover Osiris from death and restore him to life. In Egypt, Isis too saves her lover Horus, from having been ravaged to death by reconstituting him and restoring his vital powers. Just as every woman must descend into her own unconsciousness to find her authentic self and true powers within, so the Goddess on a cosmic level descends into the underworld to reclaim energy and mythically transforms death to rebirth.

In both the ancient Asian and European traditions, the role of the Great Mother Goddess was that of the divine Creatrix, the giver of life and the overseer of the cosmos. This kind of nature worship has its expressions in the early Sanskrit tradition of Asia and in the Eleusian Mysteries of ancient Greece. The earliest myths in both traditions attest to the power of the feminine creative energy in terms of what is manifested and unmanifested. The existence of goddess-centered religions and cultures uncovers the Goddess' prominent role in the establishment of moral order. As the giver and taker of life, she is also the mediator between forces.

In the ancient world, goddess mythologies were our earliest means of understanding the order of life and the genesis of the universe. The role of the Great Mother Goddess is prominent in establishing cosmic relations as affirming moral order and being the giver of life. The earliest civilizations were centered on the "Triple Goddess," so called because of her three phases as nymph, maiden, and crone corresponding to the three seasons of spring, summer, and winter. Since the reproductive cycles of plants and animals are governed by these seasons, she is also identified as Mother Earth. Her rituals included celebrations of nature and offerings of plants and herbs to the source of creation as the divine Creatrix.

The story of the Goddess is not a little complicated. Even more complicated is the significance of our loss of the sense of oneness with the universe that her presence provided. Today, we have lost sight of the ancient gynocentric belief in a living universe that sees all things as interconnected and alive. In this chapter, we will see how the formation of goddess worship and myth in matriarchal societies functioned as a living *telos*, and how the arrival and subsequent dominance of a patriarchal culture significantly altered our understanding of the universe and our sense of morality and justice.

The notion of justice as a dynamic, cosmic principle, alive and divine, and manifest in nature is part of the great mythical and historical heritage of both ancient Greece and India. The archaic age (eighth to fifth century BCE) which viewed all reality as alive and divine, on closer examination is seen to be comprised of two competing worldviews. One was the masculine aristocratic and militaristic culture, which came into ascendancy with the arrival of the Aryans. This worldview later developed into a dominant patriarchal culture of norms and laws that provides the basis for our modern-day conception of justice as an abstract principle. The older view (the one that we have almost forgotten) was rooted in the early goddess religions of the nature-based culture of the indigenous farming communities whose worship centered on the Triple Goddess because of her association with nature (the seasons, the moon, regeneration, immanence, and transcendence).[4] This kind of worship formed the basis for a matriarchal and gynocentric worldview that saw the universe as an organic whole.

The situation in the Aegean basin, the cradle of Greek thought, paralleled in many ways that of early India, which in the late Neolithic Age saw a migration of seminomadic herding, androcratic-warrior Aryans into an area whose indigenous population was primarily agricultural and gynocentric. These two cultures were in direct conflict with each other, and for the next few centuries, a constant struggle emerged as the indigenous matriarchal culture attempted to preserve its customs, myths, and ways of life in the face of constant invasion. Eventually, the patriarchal culture came to dominate in both regions, as goddess worship went underground. Thus, we can see the mixture of both cultures in the stories and myths of gods and goddesses of the pantheons of ancient Greece and India. Thereby, the religious focus shifted then from that which is immanent in nature to the transcendent sky gods. The ancient myths as they survive today, as well as later versions, represent this shifting role of the great Creatrix Goddess as she was merged and subsumed into the invaders' pantheons.

The earliest religion of the ancient Greeks was centered on the worship of a single Triple Goddess. Since the reproductive cycles of plants and animals are governed by these seasons, she was also identified as the Great Mother Earth. Justice, in its earliest religious-mythical origins, was one of the faces of the Great Mother Goddess. The function of justice as a goddess was to judge humans, either to punish or reward conduct in relation to the divine principle. This may be called the "religious face" of justice. We also know that quite a different notion of justice became explicit in classical times. It was centered on human law and was most clearly articulated by Plato and Aristotle; it changed everything. In Homeric mythology, the notion of justice as a regulative principle or law, which encompasses the social and moral order of human affairs, emerges after the face of justice as the goddess. Homer preserves this tradition of the primal Mother Goddess under the guise of "Fate." It is she who rules the universe and whose power binds both humans and gods. Her power, if ignored or challenged, brings retribution. Thus, Themis and Dikē represent a force higher than the law, and higher even than the decisions of the gods.[5]

By way of contrast, the Homeric notion of justice as law or judicial decree finds its philosophical expression in Plato and Aristotle as a universal ideal or standard of virtue. Their worldview, however, stands in contrast with the earlier indigenous culture worship of the "Great Mother" which, "was utterly different from the masculine, Homeric relationships between man and god and its shadowy, bloodless life and death."[6] Thus, along with "justice" as an abstract law or ideal, there was another Justice, very much alive. Take, for example, the myth of the goddess, Athena: J. E. Harrison rightly described the story of Athena's birth from Zeus's head as "a desperate theological expedient to rid her of matriarchal conditions. It is also a dogmatic insistence on wisdom as a male prerogative; hitherto the Goddess alone had been wise."[7]

Originally, all of the images of Athena were those of an unadorned woman whose peaceful character, wisdom, and nurturing heart were symbolized by the olive branch and the owl. It was not until Phidias portrayed her as a warrior in the great cult-statue, which he made for the Parthenon at Athens, that the conventional image of Athena became that of a woman's head surmounted by a war helmet and not as the peaceful protectress, as was her original role. Thus, it would appear that the ancient cult of the Mother Goddess as Athena was tolerated by the Greeks at this price: she must be born of Zeus alone, she must be "Zeus's obedient mouthpiece, and deliberately suppress her [true] antecedents. She employs priests, not priestesses."[8] Her power as a cosmological principle is in essence denied, as she was reduced to serving patriarchal ends as war and love goddess.

The first recorded appearance of Justice as a divine personage occurred in Hesiod's *Theogony* wherein, drawing not only on the socioreligious consciousness of his time but also on many of the earlier cult-religions, he described the forces of the universe as cosmic divinities. Hesiod portrayed

Dikē as the daughter of Zeus and Themis (daughter of Uranus and Gaia) with her other siblings, Horea (Hours), Eunomia (Order), and Eirene (Peace). Dikē executed the law of judgments and sentencing and, together with her mother Themis, carried out the final decisions of Moira.[9] For Hesiod, Justice is at the center of religious and moral life, who, independently of Zeus, is the embodiment of divine will.[10] It is important to note that Hesiod, Moira, Themis, and Dikē are the divine descendants of the Great Mother Goddess. This personification of Dikē will stand in contrast to justice viewed as custom or law and as retribution or sentence.[11]

It is with Solon that the laws of the king/state first become codified, and justice is no longer seen as aspect of the living earth Mother Goddess but as the superimposition of human law. Dikē comes to be seen in the workings of human affairs within the context of law, as universally applied equality.[12] However, as Martin Heidegger has pointed out, if Dikē is taken for the modern abstract term "justice," that is, as moral or judicial, this misses the original metaphysical sense of that ancient Greek word.[13]

It is among the natural philosophers that an understanding of justice as a distinct power first appears. In Anaximander's most notable fragment, we see the notion of cosmic justice: "according to necessity; for they pay penalty and retribution to each other for their injustice according to the assessment of time."[14] Anaximander's notion of retribution in a harmonious universe requires a sense of cosmic measure, so that all things are ordered according to their proper limits and set by cosmic balance and equilibrium. Anaximander's cosmology has its fundamental roots in mythological representation. This primal order, which for Anaximander is essentially moral, was not originally intended in any judicial sense, but rather with reference to the elements in the cosmic whole as the necessary way of nature. As Heidegger points out in his commentary on Anaximander's fragment, we are accustomed to translate "Dikē" as "right" and as that which is "out of joint." But as Heidegger asks, "But where are there jointures in what is present? . . . Or where is there even one jointure? How can what is present without jointure be out of joint?"[15]

In the Pre-Socratics, justice is seen as a cosmological and ontological necessity, not simply within human affairs but within the structure of the universe itself, as nature. Parmenides, Anaximander, and Heraclitus all speak in some way of the balance of forces, the harmony of opposites, and, in at least one instance (Parmenides), the necessity of retribution. This ancient conception as the mystical morality where Dikē means the way of righteousness is such that "all living things are under the universal sway of Dikē." Dikē then, as encompassing the whole order of nature, is the very measure of Being and, as Heidegger points out, "Dikē is the overpowering Order."[16]

The notion or understanding of justice as an overpowering order can best be described in the Parmenidean notion of the All through which all things have Being. In Parmenides, we find not simply the idea of justice, but Justice Herself. For Parmenides, Justice is seen as the divine face of the Great Mother Goddess, and this provides the necessary constraints for the realization of our inherent identity with the One. It is Justice who holds the keys to the gates of enlightenment. In the feminine symbolism of Parmenides' poem, we find, especially in the person of the Goddess, that Parmenides attests to and is a defender of the values of the Neolithic subculture, which was in danger of being further eclipsed by the nascent scientific outlook being propagated by the Pythagorean movement.[13] As a result, the face of justice as the Triple Goddess was lost in the European tradition. Hence, gone are the days when not even the sun dared to step out of its measure.

We also find the mystical notion of measure and harmony in the Asian tradition, specifically, in the Vedas, in concept of Rta as "what is adjusted, fitted together."[18] The Vedic notion of Rta emerges in the early hymns of the *Rig Veda* as the standard of justice, as cosmic order or eternal law, and it helps to form the foundation of the ethical claim of dharma. Rta is not personified as one of the gods/goddesses of Vedic mythology but is repeatedly recognized in hymns to Agni and Varuna (the dispenser of law) as righteousness or the unity of reality. Rta, literally understood as "the course of things," represents the eternal law of the universe. Virtue, then, is conformity to the cosmic law.[17] The concept of Rta as the unity of nature's order was instrumental in providing the early Vedic thinkers with a regulative principle of cosmic order and righteousness that later would merge into a comprehensive morality. The role of Rta as a regulative moral principle came to be symbolized in the recurrent activities of nature as "what holds together."[18]

In India, Justice is seen as a function within the role and symbolism of the Great Mother traditions. The early prehistory of India corresponds in many ways with that of ancient Greece, where again the Aryans ("the people of sky") invaded the early matriarchal gynocentric culture of the Dravidians. Here we can see the similarities in terms of their matriarchal beliefs and rituals in their Paleolithic caves and mounds. The earliest Great Mother cults of Asia were earth-centered, focusing on fertility and life-giving energy. Their rituals included celebrations of nature and the offering of plants and herbs to the source of creation. With the conquest of the Aryans, the religious focus shifted from that which was immanent in nature to the transcendent sky gods with rituals involving fire and smoke. The early goddess religions attempted to assimilate the patriarchal gods into their culture and, for some time after the initial invasion, the Goddess was worshipped as one of the primary deities. Yet, as was the situation in ancient Greece, this adaptation soon gave way to the superimposition of patriarchal gods and resulted in the conception of Brahman as ultimate reality. With the conquest of the Aryans, however, Rta as the way of nature became subsumed under the law of karma. The role of Rta as a regulative moral principle symbolized the recurrent activities of humans and nature. Thus, we can see the importance of Rta for the ethical formulation of the dharma.

The Vedic and early Buddhist schools have much the same notion as that of the ancient Greeks, where justice, as dharma/karma, is a living ethical force inherent in the structure and creation of the universe. In the Asian schools of nondualism, Maya is traditionally understood as illusion, as unreality. However, Maya is also the World Mother, identical to Brahman, and is understood as manifesting and partially revealing various levels of Being. Maya also has the connotation of discrimination or measure: from the root "*ma*," "to measure, to form, to build."[19] In Maya, we find the image of the World Mother as the cosmic "second," which conceals and reveals all divine experience. She is the discerner and judge as to whether the one seeking enlightenment is deserving of the full truth. There are innumerable manifestations of this play of Maya as the World Mother. As the second, she expresses "the mode of divine dualistic experience."[20] She is the triple goddess Shakti-Maya-Devi, mythically recognized and understood as the "mother of all Life Energy." Our present state of ignorance and bondage is due to the illusion of Maya's creative energy, and yet, were this energy absent, existence would not be possible. Accordingly, it is through Shakti-Maya-Devi that we realize our essential identity. Swami Muktananda, in his book *Play of Consciousness*, pays homage to the goddess Shakti as the discerner and sustainer of the whole universe. Shakti Kundalini is beyond dualistic distinctions. She is both the perceiver and that which is perceived "the perceivable universe is the outer expression of Her inner pulsation."[21] Ultimately, good and evil belong to Shakti-Maya-Devi. Maya, then, like Dikē, both reveals and conceals the divine One, but She is also that same One.

Mythically understood, the Great Mother Goddess generates all forms and is identified with Vishnu's second wife, the earth (bhumi) or with nature/matter (prakti). She can appear in many forms in natural phenomena or in human form as wife, mother, young girl, or old woman. Some of her main representations are as Durga, the "difficult to access" slayer of the buffalo demon; as Kali, the warrior who personifies the wrath of women; and as consorts or energies of the gods, particularly, Sarasvati, Parvathi, and Lakshmi. These representations tell us that Shakti-Maya-Devi is matter (praktri), power (shakti), creative illusion (maya) and the worldly cycle itself (samsara). Shakta "thealogy" describes a Mother Goddess who encompasses light and sound, name and form, purity and impurity, what is auspicious and what is inauspicious, creation and destruction. Binding all beings, her power both enslaves and liberates. She is Shakti, the divine energy that generates all forms. She is accessible, immanent, and worldly. She absorbs all Shakti(s) into herself. For her devotees, she is the ultimate reality who embraces the totality of what is.

The examples from the abovementioned mythical representations tell us that the Great Mother Goddess not only takes on many feminine forms to form a great Goddess but also indicates what the great Goddess has inside her which creates her nature as that which is beyond form. The most prominent form the feminine principle takes is as the consort of Shiva. This Shakti-Shiva (female/male energy) is the personification of the dynamic and dyadic powers of being and becoming, actuality and potentiality. Yet, as we learn, this polarity is not a mere balance of opposites. The Shakti principle as feminine energy is what is essential for all life. Vishnu dreams the dream of creation and his power lies coiled, dormant, asleep. The male power is inert, passive, and requires female energy to awaken it. Without female kinetic energy, there is no creation and no evolution.

In Tibetan Buddhism, we find the notion of the "Mother of the Buddhas" (Prajnapararnita), "Womb of the Reality." One of the more meaningful points that have arisen from the feminist analysis of Buddhism has been the emphasis on the interconnectedness and dynamic of all reality. Here, the Earth Mother is seen as essential emptiness, which is the basis for all identity and relation. While the Buddhists would readily recognize that the basic ground is neither male nor female, the symbolism is meant to refer to the feminine principle of creativity and birth, or, perhaps more specifically, as pure potentiality or empty space. It should be noted that, just as Maya is not mere illusion, the Primordial Mother of Tantric Buddhism is not mere emptiness. Emptiness is the ground of all possibilities, of enlightenment, of life, of interdependence.[22] All things are the "active play of the female creative principle."[23] The womb of life is the measure of all things. In Tantric thought, "creation is time" and Maya's function as measurer is to weave the substance of events.[24] The Great Mother principle is considered through her symbolism and her creative powers to be the source of all dharmas. As such, she not only creates good and evil but is their very manifestation. Her's is not only the gate of birth but also the dharma gate of enlightenment itself, the perfection of "profound cognition." The principle of judgment based on the primordial emptiness/fullness of Being is present within the essence of the Great Mother. Here she is the lawgiver, the order of time, and judge of Being. As the primordial mother of all life energy, her justice, like that of the ancient Greeks, is organic and alive.

We have seen that, if we trace the roots of justice to its early mythical Indo-European sources, we find the face of the Triple Goddess in both traditions. The prehistorical sources agree that one of the functions of the Great Cosmic Mother is as the guardian, manifestation, and mediations of being. This is where I believe the concept of measure occurs in both traditions. The body of the Great Mother is not separate from the universe. She is the very measure of Being. As the judge and discerner of reality, one of her functions is to balance the polarity of opposites, being and nonbeing, reality and illusion, good and evil. As we have also seen, the Great Mother Goddess is portrayed in both cultures as the "gate keeper," to truth, enlightenment, being, and nonbeing. She is the giver of life and, as such is the lawgiver. This was one of the original faces of Justice. Her law is the law of creation and cannot be superimposed as an objective standard; indeed, her law is beyond convention where Dikē is the avenging force of Fate, and Kali wears a necklace of human skulls to remind us of the didactic power of creation. In ancient Greece, the ordinance of the Goddess superseded even Zeus, and in India, it was Earth Mother herself who sanctioned the Buddha's enlightenment. Accordingly, she is the judge of all, and, in both traditions, Her decrees are seen as necessarily inviolate. In the *Great Cosmic Mother*, Sjöö and Mor state, "this form of the Goddess is always the law giver, the order of time, the judge of the dead the eternal source of wisdom and ecstasy."[25]

As the primordial mother of all life energy, her justice is alive and divine. Regulatory principles prescribed by society miss the mark of integration, interconnection, and embodiment, and they fragment Being from itself. It is extraordinary how current ideas of justice have become so distorted from their ancient conceptions. In both traditions, justice has its philosophical source in the embodiment of the Divine Mother. The principles derived from such a manifestation are based on the ancient monist/nondualistic understanding of the interconnection and relation of all reality, the oneness of what is. The prepatriarchal nature of justice as the Great Mother is not the polar opposite of the patriarchal god. She is, in principle, beyond all opposites, containing them within herself. Her justice demands that we take the duality of nature as primordial emptiness or unity. Part of her triple function is severe and horrific, as the force of avenging Justice. This is the "dark side" of the Mother. This side of the Great Mother is veiled, hidden, concealed. She is not referred to as "dark" to indicate color or evil, but rather to stress the primal nature of her being, that which is unmanifested. She is the force, which adjusts internal relations to the external world.

We have lost sight of the origin and ontological function of justice as the embodiment of being, as inherent in the nature of the cosmos itself. Today, justice as a regulating principle is that which is superimposed through religion, culture, and nationalism, as a conception of duty or as a mere abstraction. We seek justice outside ourselves in government, in courts, in god, and in religion. This is a far cry from justice as a way of being, justice as alive, justice as cosmological. Its living center is embedded not only in the energies of nature and the universe but also in our hearts and minds and in our prepatriarchal, primordial spirit-body. The Goddess's gynocentric powers of fertility, creation, destruction, and connection to the earth are symbolized powerfully in her role as Justice both in Greek and Indian philosophy. The ancient philosophers upheld the idea that the nature of the world was indeed a moral order. Human's wrongdoings impact nature and nature responds to human beings because all living beings are part of Her. Further, the moral order of nature mandates that not one thing go beyond its limitations, its measure; domination of another is by definition unjust. Matriarchal notions of justice reflect spiritual and cosmological rather than political or military structures. For example, consider the fact that the deity as giver of life was replaced with a male tribal god. Because the warring tribal culture recognized that men through battle could take life, the premise for first principles changed from justice, necessity and nature to fear and greed. Since then, patriarchal war gods have been warring for centuries. The place of honor, which was originally held by the giver of life, was replaced, by way of violence and domination, with a throne of power for the taker of life.

The ancient belief in the inherent order of Nature as the law of life stands in contrast to our modern separation of society and nature where rules apply merely to the social order and do not incorporate any sense of cosmic justice. Instead, anthropomorphic deities form the standards of morality, where death becomes life and war is holy. Modern societies based on patriarchal religions and myths of power have turned away from the ancient archaic values and, as a result of losing and repressing female energies, are now on a path of global self-destruction. As Mary Daly writes, the women's movement is "the greatest single hope for survival of spiritual consciousness on this planet."[26] And that spiritual consciousness is not separate from how we live. Women's energies can create a new world order: a biophilic ethic, a return to a living justice. Patriarchal rules, cultures, religions, and superstitions have enslaved our minds for centuries, teaching us to think a certain way, behave a certain way, and be a certain way, that is, to cooperate with plan of the "fathers." Ultimately, however, women have allowed this thinking to enslave themselves.

It is a matter of conscious responsibility and self-liberation for us to reexamine our radical roots in Goddess worship. The notion that the Mother Goddess holds the powers of nature does more than simply suggest her connection to the earth and cosmos. From the sacredness of spinning and weaving found in Old Europe, to her role as giver of life and overseer of the cosmos, the existence of goddess-centered religions and cultures uncovers the Goddess' prominent role in the establishment, not only of life but also of moral order and responsibility. While the majority of feminist work on the Great Mother cults focuses on Her embodiment and interconnection with nature, her status actually guarantees cosmic order, meta-cosmic relations, and meta-cosmic justice. The Goddess stands for necessity and righteousness in nature. She who gives life determines first principles. She lays the foundations for a dynamic biophilic ethic, rather than a stagnant and codified moral code.

Today, feminist philosophers are attempting to reconstruct a feminist vision of a global ethics and ecojustice. The ancient religions of the Great Mother tradition, which celebrated the female form and power to create is hidden in the rituals, ideologies, myths, and doctrines of the present. Her presence in rituals in world religions allows us to experience the primal connection between the human and divine. It is no surprise that the universe was originally represented in female imagery. Her presence is perhaps what can alleviate the concurrent problems of corruption, destruction, superimposition, and its corresponding corollary of idolatry. The face of Justice as the Great Mother stands prior to all patriarchal articulations and reflects a nondualistic and biophilic expanse necessary for a global community.

Ancient goddess worship provides the basis for a biophilic ethic by establishing the ground of the oneness of all beings and things as essentially alive. The whole of nature will teach us about balance and proper relations within the All. The essential nature of justice, unlike what Plato has taught us, is not an abstract transcendental ideal separate from the earth, but rather a force of nature itself. The earth is alive, and as we seek to establish the embodiment of the principles of a living oneness, justice too comes alive. However, first, we must recognize the importance of what we have lost in negating the sense of the universe as a living oneness.

NOTES

1. Waltert Burket, *Greek Religion*, trans. John Raffan (Cambridge, MA: Harvard University Press, 1989), 22 351n. Burket offers up the dominant opinion that "Matriarchy in the true sense has not been shown to have existed anywhere in the Aegean of Near Eastern pre-history."

2. Marija Gimbutas, *The Gods and Goddesses of Old Europe* (London: Thames and Hudson, 1974).

3. Mircea Eliade, *Myths, Dreams and Mysteries*, trans. Philip Mairet (New York: Harper Torchbooks, 1960), 27.

4. W. K. C Guthrie, *The Greeks and Their Gods* (Boston: Beacon Press, 1955), 30.

5. Richard Cunliffe, *A Lexicon of Homeric Dialect* (Norman and London: University of Oklahoma Press, 1988). In its earliest religious-mythical origins, justice was one of the faces of the great Goddess. The oldest "recorded" appearance of justice in ancient Greece is found in the *Iliad* and *Odyssey* of Homer. Homer uses the Greek words "*Dikē*" and "*themis*" to designate "custom" or "way of behavior," which accords with what is ordained by law, with an emphasis on human decrees. Thus, there is to be found in Homeric mythology, the notion of justice as a regulative

principle or law and also the former tradition of justice as a face of the primal Mother Goddess.

6. W.K.C. Guthrie, *The Birth of Western Civilization* (New York: McGraw-Hill, 1964), 1086.

7. Marija Gimbutas, *The Language of the Goddess* (San Francisco: Harper and Row, 1989), 46.

8. Ibid., 47.

9. Julius Stone, *Human Law and Human Justice* (Stanford: Stanford University Press, 1965), 10.

10. Werner Jaeger, *Paideia: The Ideals of Greek Culture*, trans. Gilbert Highet (New York: Oxford University Press, 1962), 59–71.

11. Donna, Giancola, "Justice and the Face of the Great Mother, East and West," *Proceedings from the 20th World Congress of Philosophy, Paideia: Philosophy Educating Humanity*, 2001.

12. Ibid., 62, 104.

13. Martin, Heidegger, *An Introduction to Metaphysics*, trans. Ralph Manheim (New Haven: Yale University Press, 1959), 160.

14. Forrest Baird and Walter Kaufmann, *Ancient Philosophy*, 2nd ed. Vol. 1 (New Jersey: Prentice Hall, 1997), 9.

15. Martin Heidegger, *Early Greek Thinking*, trans. David Farrell Kell and Frank Capuzzi (San Francisco: Harper and Row Publishers, 1984), 41.

16. Martin, Heidegger, *An Introduction to Metaphysics*, 165.

17. Sarvepalli Radhakrishnan, and Charles Moore, *A Source Book in Indian Philosophy* (Princeton: Princeton University Press, 1973), 25.

18. M. Hiriyana, *The Essentials of Indian Philosophy* (London: George Allen and Unwin LTD, 1969), 37.

19. Heinrich Zimmer, *Philosophies of India* (New York: Meridian Books, 1957), 19.

20. Ibid., 460.

21. Muktananda, *Play of Consciousness* (New York: Syda Foundation, 1978), xxi–xxvi.

22. Anne Klein, *Meeting the Great Bliss Queen* (Boston: Beacon Press, 1995), 159.

23. Monica Sjöö, and Barbara Mor, *The Great Cosmic Mother* (New York: Harper Collins Publishers, 1991), 221.

24. Ibid., 222.

25. Ibid., 155.

26. Mary Daly, *Beyond God the Father* (Boston: Beacon Press, 1985), 14.

Chapter 2

Falling Down Patriarchy

An examination of our dominant patriarchal paradigm will reveal that the philosophical underpinnings of our institutions and practices are woefully destructive, dualistic with a vengeance, and ultimately, self-destructive. Modern-day patriarchal systems of domination have provided the basis for such problems as globalization, exploitation, starvation, ecological destruction, and loss of biodiversity, to name only a few. It is my contention that patriarchy cannot endure as a self-sustaining system, and, therefore, any ethical theory of social or ecological justice and sustainability must necessarily arise within a meta-patriarchal context. The feminist movement has already offered scathing critiques of the domination and oppression of women and nature by patriarchy. Following those observations, this chapter will offer a brief comparison and contrast of the principles of matriarchy and patriarchy and, in so doing, underscore the philosophical assumption of dualism inherent within our ethical traditions.

In spite of all of the achievements in the twenty-first century, we must admit that something is terribly wrong. As much as we may appreciate the comforts of our postmodern society, it is at odds with itself and, a greater problem still, it is at odds with life in general. The path along which civilization has proceeded has led those who share in its so-called progress, the globalized industrialized nations of the world, to unparalleled wealth of resources, power, and technology. And in this process, as Carl Jung describes it, "western man" has become "assiduous, fearful, devout, self-abasing, enterprising, greedy and violent in his pursuit of the goods of world."[1] Further, instead of being in balance with whole, the negative traits of patriarchal civilization have doubled and erupted into unspeakable social injustices and ecological destruction.

In response, world religions have fallen short in addressing the atrocities and hypocrisies committed on social levels, even in those religions that claim to be socially engaged. Instead, they have helped frame systems of domination and have given power to abusive practices of globalization. From a religious perspective, nature is typically seen as sacred. Yet, the earth and her resources are being depleted and destroyed in "his" name. Environmental movements have not stemmed from traditional religious groups, but instead from secular and educated groups. Religious ideals of purity and cleanliness, apparently, are not in line with the ecological concerns for a clean and sustainable environment. In promoting patriarchal propaganda, world religious institutions have done little to address the growing concerns for life on this planet. For the most part, they have remained strangely quiet about climate change, social injustices, and the role of women in general (except when it comes to controlling women's bodies). World religions have become the minions of global institutions, policies, and patriarchal practices that defile life rather than uplift it.

Patriarchal myths of globalization and the fallout from industrialized agriculture affect everything, from soybeans to shrimp and from salmon to cows creating a massive upheaval of indigenous communities and nonhuman beings that are grossly altered and destroyed by industrialized agriculture and massive global corporations and institutions. Through globalization, the destruction of the environment, food security, land, and local economies has been destroyed systematically.[2] Developing countries have suffered from environmental issues, such as deforestation and pollution, and have blamed westernization and modernization for destroying the traditional sense of unity between humans and nature. This is the classical colonization story, where the seeds of racism and greed spread their sickness and corrupt economies, food systems, local farming, health, spiritual connections, and natural ecosystems of hundreds of thousands of people who lived and survived before the global systems where forced upon them.

There is a direct link between world institutions and organizations and the suffering of local communities infected by patriarchal organizations. Globalization is a sanctioned way in which local people are dominated and subjugated by global companies and institutions in pursuit of homogeneity and monopolization. Globalization as the birthchild of patriarchy has its roots in imperialism and colonization. Global organizations and entities such as the World Bank, the World Trade Organization, and the Brenton Woods Act are another wave of colonization and have negatively impacted agriculture, land use, natural resources, women, and wildlife.

For example, according to the World Health Organization, approximately 2.1 billion individuals across the globe have a limited access to clean water every day.[3] The responsibility of providing water in homes is often on girls and women, more so in rural parts. In most parts of the world, they are traditionally responsible for hygiene, sanitation, and other water uses, and this mandates them to collect water from rivers and streams that are far away from their homes. These tasks increase their susceptibility to violence and reduce the time for other things, including attending school or income-generating endeavors. As such, access to clean water presents detrimental effects to women.

In terms of land resources, ever since the British colonization period, land access and ownership has shifted from sustainable community-based models of ownership, tenure, and use to a feudal one. The result is that a very elite minority holds title to most of a country's arable land. Workers are alienated from the benefits of their labor, which in turn reduces the productivity of land and relegates the majority of the population to almost utter poverty. Further, land reform movements in developing countries have proven to exasperate inequalities rather than decreasing them.[4]

Global industrialization was first marketed as a necessary means to prevent poverty and starvation. Under the guise of betterment, globalized corporations falsely claim that they aim to increase food security or that genetically modified seeds are superior to traditional grown seeds. In this manner, they destroy local and national markets, which lead not only to environmental destruction but also to the removal of the people's relationship with the nature. For example, corporations like Monsanto that hold patents on seeds create problems and then sell the solutions. By patenting hybrid seeds that are more susceptible to pests, they then sell pesticides as well. Then, they sell new hybrid seeds resistant to pesticides. Farmers thus risk losing all their crops unless they purchase more seeds. This process creates economic hardship and the very same food insecurity that these corporations claim they are attempting to solve.[5] In conjunction with over-farming and the loss of biodiversity, rural and indigenous people have lost their livelihood and their culture in favor of the promise of production.

Global corporations are impoverishing the earth by acquiring resources, polluting, and overusing limited supplies. They disrupt local economies and by maldistribution further the gap between rich and poor. Throughout all structures of domination in the world, there is one common feature: the subjugation, exploitation, and oppression of women and nature. Thus, the domination of women, the domination of the economy, which, as Luce Irigaray claims, is basically a homosexual economy based on the exchanges of goods between men,[6] and the domination of the environment produce interlocking systems of domination.

Among the many forms of subjection, exploitation, and pollution of our natural resources, there is one that remains so elusive that we dare not speak its name: the pollution of the human mind/spirit.[7] Patriarchal myths of power, cloaked in what Judith Butler refers to as the language of kingship[8] and authority, reinforce and manipulate all levels of discourse and thinking. This manipulation makes it hard to challenge the underlying assumption that patriarchy is the righteous, natural, and god-given way for a just society to proceed.[9] Indeed, buttressed by male monotheistic religions, patriarchy encloses itself and everything else off from the whole of being. Fragmenting and rupturing humans from the world of nature, and from each other, patriarchy creates an ethos devoid of an authentic ontological and spiritual source, totally removed from the primordial oneness.[10]

One of the great illusions perpetrated and perpetuated by patriarchy is dualism. The problem with dualism as an underlying mode of thought is that it fragments reality from itself, humans from nature and each other, and it removes the living spirit from the living world, rarefying it into a static and fixed absolute without life. The most basic form that dualism takes is metaphysical dualism: the belief that there are two separate kinds of substances: spirit and matter. This metaphysical divide, present in all western religious traditions, conjures a split consciousness of reality, where things, beings, and ideas are regulated to their appropriate domain. God is removed from the earth, nature is viewed merely as matter, and as a commodity for consumption and capital gain, and the soul and body are treated as distinct entities. Another form of dualism, epistemological dualism, separates the self from others and maintains that this separation is an effect of human consciousness and projection, creating an inevitable category of "other." But "otherness" is not a natural state. We are not born with it, it is artificially imposed and conditioned unto us. Humans, indeed all living beings, become divided from each other according to arbitrary classifications, while ethical and cultural imperialism gives way to all sorts of social, classist, and ethical distinctions in the fiber of our everyday lives. Social and ecological injustices and inequities are justified and upheld by bifurcated thinking.

A dualistic perspective divides and conquers. Ever since Plato, the western world has been under the sway of division. It appears that we have not recovered from Plato and his world of transcendent illusions. Predating Plato, Parmenides, a fifth-century BCE philosopher, warned us against going down the way of "opposing stress," where being and nonbeing are seen as one and the same. As Parmenides, instructs us, the "all is full of the what is." Being is everywhere, it is all that is, and it is alive. For Parmenides, as for many of the ancient philosophers, being was seen as one, an organic primordial whole; not separate from natural world, but inherent in it.[11]

The earliest philosophers of the ancient Greek world understood the primordial oneness of nature and sought causal answers within the unity and order of the universe, the cosmos itself, without going beyond it. What most scholars today consider an archaic and naive explanation reveals instead a cosmological and metaphysical understanding of the one being that manifests itself in and through the multitude of natural phenomena.[12] However, with the emergence of the *logos* or reason came the first veil of human rationality, superimposing its own logic on the world of nature.[13] Layer upon layer of more supposedly advanced theories finally give way to a construction of various orders of reality, removing both the natural and the human from direct contact with whole.

It is with Plato that life ultimately and finally gets split off from its source and placed in a different realm altogether. For Plato, the world of ideas or forms stands apart from the natural world and is the only proper object of knowledge. According to Plato, the realm of the forms is transcendent, unchanging, static, and separate from life. Entities existing independently from the human mind, void of matter, nature, life, and mind, Plato insists, are completely real. This is the world of being for Plato. Philosophically speaking, this is the final cut for removing truth from life. The natural world or the world of becoming, which Parmenides referred to as the "mixed way," of confusing being and non-being, is for Plato a mere a shadow of the real, not part of a larger whole. Thus, for Plato, and subsequently for most of Western thought, mind and body are separate entities, each with its own realm, while the life of man-made reason is seen as superior to any lived reality. Is it any wonder, then, that we are at war with ourselves, with each other and nature in general?

From a pragmatic perspective, one may be tempted to claim that the problems of patriarchy, racism, and sexism associated with the traditions and religions of the west are not present in the Asian traditions of nondualism in schools of religious thought, such as Hinduism, Buddhism, and Taoism. Here, I cannot resist asking whether the sins of patriarchy are any different or better without the assumption of dualism? To be sure, the philosophical recognition of the pervasive oneness, or nonduality, of the real allows for a radical and liberating way to see beyond conventional distinctions of self and other, matter and spirit, etc. Yet, in spite of this recognition, women, animals, and the planet are not faring any better. The assumption of dualism invades and pervades our consciousness in common everyday thinking: from household chores, childrearing and basic sustenance to labor force, social status, and economic security. Even in fundamentally nondualistic traditions, there remains a wide chasm and imbalance between male and female, in terms of theory and practice, social and cultural norms, legal and political institutions, spiritual development, and personal autonomy and responsibility. One needs only to carry out a quick examination into the status of women worldwide to see that gender inequality is pervasive regardless of metaphysical or religious differences.[14] In fact, the Food and Agriculture Organization (FAO) of the United Nations has adopted gender equality as major goal because women, land, and sustainability are intimately interwoven.[15]

In the Asian traditions of nondualism, in schools of Hinduism and Buddhism, for example, the role of women, even though revered in a theoretical sense, is deemed lower and less entitled to rights, protections, and personal and civil liberties. While ultimately a spiritual understanding of the unity of all things collapses, distinctions between matter and spirit, self and other, male and female, and gender inequalities still play out in practice. Even though the goddess has been revered for centuries in many Asian traditions and is still worshiped as one of the primary deities in many localities, her role was regulated by the emergence of Brahman as the ultimate reality. Hence, eclipsing her power by patriarchal gods.

It has even been debated whether or not women are even capable of enlightenment. One only need be reminded of the caste system where the status of women under law in India is controlled by men. Until recently, women were not even allowed to inherit property. And in Buddhism, where again gender discrimination should not even exist, instances of gender inequality range from the status of women as the result of negative karma, to the *Jataka* tales of the Buddha's previous incarnations as exclusively male.[16] The Buddha is recorded as having been reluctant to allow women into the order of the *Sangha*, claiming it would diminish the influence of Buddhism by 500 years. Even today, not only are there pitifully few female spiritual leaders but also the rules and power structures of religious organizations repeat the practices of male spiritual superiority. Nowhere is woman's spiritual authority or personal autonomy viewed as equal to her male counterpart.

In would seem then, regardless of over-arching metaphysical beliefs and doctrines, in practice, women are regulated to the role of "other," as inferior beings.[17] Perceived as more closely aligned with natural world than the world of man-made reason, almost nowhere are women seen as equal to men.[18] Patriarchal beliefs in duality remain dominant and create false constructions, regulating women and nature as a repository for male "otherness."

As long as we operate under a binary architectonic, the stress of opposition and, ultimately, superiority and suppression come into play. Matriarchy versus patriarchy, male versus female, self versus other, feminism versus everything else . . . these are binary wars of power based on false dichotomies and views of opposition and domination.[19] The philosophical assumption of dualism inherent within western ethical traditions has proven fatal to nature, women, all indigenous peoples, and the planet in general. World religions and global politics reinforce the schisms that separate and fragment ourselves from the whole.

In spite of all of the efforts on behalf of international human rights in protecting our environment, current thinking is still imperialist, paternalistic, and misogynistic.[20] Laws and regulations do nothing to alleviate the stress, themselves being the by-product of patriarchal law codes. From an historical perspective, the origin of law is patriarchy. Complex law codes are firmly established in all meta-cosmic religions and their cultures.[21] Accordingly, they are said to be ordained by authority (male or divine male), eternal, immutable, and not subject to human will. Their violation results in moral condemnation and punishment. Justice becomes codified as a set of standardized abstract principles. They are, in fact, androcentric principles, arbitrarily created and enforced to promote the status of male superiority at the expense of women, indigenous peoples, and nature. Social, religious, and political norms promote the exploitation of nature and gender so that inequality may remain dominant. Thus, feminist objections to patriarchal conceptions of law are based on the androcentric insistence of universality of the male, disregard for human emotions and empathy, and the tyranny of abstract principles over concrete relations and interconnections. Any attempt to put forth a new code of ethics or law codes in line with feminist principles of interconnection, sustainability, and holistic practices cannot come about without a full rejection of patriarchal norms.

The reason patriarchy will ultimately self-destruct is because it denies its own kinship with the family of all living beings. Dualism affords a society controlled by men, essentially the ability to utilize violent practices, patterns, and beliefs to dominate and destroy women, nature, animals, the planet, and now, perhaps, outer space. As modes of thought, dualism and patriarchy have enjoyed a long and insidious history together. Dualism underscores and provides patriarchy with the philosophical and ideological basis for male control and manipulation of power, land, and resources. Note that nearly all areas of life on the entire earth are inhabited, exploited, and dominated by men.

With its assumption of male superiority, patriarchy perpetuates the false dichotomy of self and other and grossly affects all other relationships regulating them to a good/evil superior/inferior opposition. As Rosemary Radford Ruether states, "evil comes about precisely by the distortion of the self-other relationships into the good-evil, superior-inferior dualism."[22] Indeed, the very category of "otherness" constitutes an evil of dualism and allows for all kinds of political injustices on behalf of male elite subjectivity. This pervasive dualism results in the gendering of knowledge and ethics, where patriarchy claims sovereignty and objectivity over all discourses and disciplines. The dualistic patriarchal assertions of a reality and knowledge of self and other correspond to a falsely imposed ethical criterion of good and evil which is the cause of our present state of alienation. Patriarchal claims of knowledge and selfhood. In short, the assumption of dualism itself is the critical pillar that we must overcome.[23]

What is lacking is what ancient people seemed to know and what moderns have lost: respect for the sacredness of life. We must look deeper into the face of nature and recognize the ultimate oneness of life, where all beings are sacred to the whole. The loss of this sense of oneness of a living universe is likewise the loss of a matriarchal worldview and effectively mutilates ourselves separating ourselves from any integrated organic living whole. This fissure occurred as a result of a religious philosophical shift from nature worship to a dualistic patriarchal theism, that is evidenced in the religious, cultural, social, political, and economic structures and localities and nations around the world. Fundamental to the shift from humanity's sense of interconnection to nature and to the rise of patriarchy is the subordination of women. Because of the perceived role of women as being connected to the nature and life cycles of living beings, women have long suffered the effects of the power of patriarchal domination. Not only has patriarchy lost contact with the oneness of all things, but it has also turned the one into the two and created the "other." This has resulted in a self-destructive imbalance between humans and nature and humans among themselves. This spiritual and existential rupture radiates injustice and discord through our modern paradigms and experiences of daily life.

Patriarchy will always fight to retain its power, quickly countering and thwarting any attempt to overthrow its dominion, depleting and devastating the earth and its resources in the process. All systems, from the microcosmic to the macrocosmic, seek to self-maintain and to preserve their internal structures. Even dysfunctional systems seek to avoid change and continue the status quo. Think of the example of family dynamics, where abuse is tolerated for the sake of perpetuating the survival of the group. The instinct for self-survival is primal in all systems, even to the point of the inevitable destruction of its own inner workings and components. The whole cannot survive without the parts, and here we have the problem with patriarchy: it is not sustainable. Patriarchy as a system (ideological, political, economic, etc.) perpetuates its own destruction by exploiting and destroying its resources. No system can withstand continual depletion of energy and resources without consuming itself. It is not self-sustaining; it is self-consuming, and thus, its value system is corrupted by its greed. What is good for the whole is not necessarily good for the parts. The whole cannot exist at the expense of the parts indefinitely. At some point, it becomes parasitical. Patriarchy turns morality upside down by proselytizing deception, and from the outset, this is most certainly immoral.

In terms of ethical systems, matriarchy is not like patriarchy, except with women in charge.[24] The Great Mother Goddess needed for ecological and social change is not the polarized "other" of the god(s) of patriarchal religions. Matriarchal societies challenge patriarchy with an entirely radical worldview. Their fundamental tenets are different and irreconcilable. The most notable distinction being the presumption and proliferation of dualism. Matriarchal societies, based on an awareness of a universal oneness, a living whole are organic, nondualistic, and uphold the sacredness of the natural world. Patriarchal societies are hierarchical so that power and wealth move from the top down. In contrast, matriarchies allow for more equitable movement within the structures, providing for a balance of power between parts within a whole. Living within patriarchal societies promotes competition across all venues, and this results in a disconnection from a greater whole as well as an egotistic mindset of personal survival. In contrast, matriarchy lends itself to a collective mindset of cooperation and interconnection between parts for the sake of the whole.

The notion of interconnection in matriarchal societies also creates a challenging orientation of the self. Under patriarchy, particularly in western ethical theories, the assumption is one of autonomous agency where the self is viewed as essentially free and independent. This assumption has led us down the falsehood of so-called objectivity, where the male mind somehow is able to grasp the true nature of reason, science, and nature, etc. This is the dominant discourse that some feminists have named "phallo-centric."[25] The notion of self in current feminist thought is viewed, not as autonomous and independent but embodied and standing in relation to others. This interconnection of self with other has plagued women who have long been treated as ethically inferior to men because of women's relational ties and connections.

Among those relationships, and of equal ethical importance, although perhaps less obvious, is how the two different worldviews see time. Time, in the modern world of patriarchy, is in commonsense fashion, linear: Beginning, Middle, End, Past, Present, and Future. Of course, the majority realizes that time is vastly more complex, but that complexity is not part of our everyday thinking. We think in terms of a time line, especially those of us educated in the west. In contrast, the ancient and prepatriarchal societies view time as cyclical: rotations and orbits, repetitive patterns of life and death, ebbing and flowing, the cycles of nature of life, death, and rebirth. This conception of time places the individual within the order of the cycles of nature and not standing outside of it. This awareness of the reoccurring life and death cycle of nature gives a sense of perspective of our place in the order of things.

In general, matriarchal societies have reverence for nature and a respect for all life-forms. They understand that our interconnection with all beings is mutual. They also differ from patriarchal counterparts in that they promote sustainability and equality by the sharing of goods throughout the community. This idea of shared goods and circulated resources in matriarchal societies is not easily transferable into patriarchal structures because of the complexity of the inherent systems of domination in the global economy. Patriarchy has created a lack and scarcity of resources, so violence and social injustices ensue. We live in a world where children are starving still. These problems occur, not just in developing countries, but on a mass scale so that economic tensions breed worldwide destruction, famine, and alienation.

For the past several centuries, and across all lands, patriarchy has created ethical systems and codified law codes that serve the purpose of men. Since long before the aqueducts patriarchy has been building and constructing. The earth, all societies, and all living creatures have been under the sway of male thought, and all have been inflicted with their new and improved vision of progress. It seems that we cannot let nature be. This domination of nature and human and nonhuman "others" is justified by an oppressive patriarchal framework characterized by a logic of domination. But is this ethical? Is the ethical even possible under patriarchy? To be sure, this meta-ethical question can only be asked and answered from beyond a patriarchal mindset.

The field of ethics itself as a product of male thought can hardly be counted on for insight.[26] Moving into a meta-patriarchal ethos requires more than a mere reformation of ideas and practices. Meta-patriarchal thinking is more than moving beyond patriarchy, making patriarchy appear as if it were the standard; it is rather a leap into a more organic mindset encompassing the meta-ethical to the everyday in learning to live justly.[27] We must move away from patriarchal conceptions of good and evil, with their accompanying social and religious schisms, into a radical understanding of our interconnection with nature. The patriarchal gods ought to be damned when basic sustenance becomes a moral and ecological crisis, when the economy is alive and cultures are dying, when life begins in the mind of man and nature becomes extinct. Fortunately, we are beginning to experience the death throes of patriarchy, although few will admit it. As soon as we as people move beyond idolatry, then some new vision for the future may appear. Such a transformation of value cannot come from within our present patriarchal mind set, with its limited, rigid, and compassion-less insistence on its own necessity and superiority, as if there were no other way of thinking. Nature is teleological and holistic, and any system of ethics must align itself with the basic conditions for the preservation for life.

The divisions that separate us from all that is are superimposed and have perpetuated the justification for the domination and destruction of this sacred earth. Defined by its category of "otherness" patriarchy thereby becomes fatal to others. We have lost the understanding of living justice as that which binds Being together as an interconnection of microcosm and macrocosm, as part of organic whole. We have allowed for abstract principles to override concrete relations, and therefore, we search for justice in every place except within ourselves. We must move beyond the category of "otherness." In dismissing harmony, balance and proper portion, and measure, we are guilty of a far greater *hubris* than we may imagine. The challenge of a biophilic ethic is the resurrection of a living justice that is embodied in all that is, humans and nonhumans, the earth, the stars, the order of the heavens. Without a living connection to the earth, we lose touch with the sacredness of life. This is not another ethical theory. It is an energetic fact: Nature will have the last word, because there is no "other."

NOTES

1. Carl Gustav Jung, *Psychology and Religion: West and East*, trans. R.F.C.P. Hull (New York: Pantheon Books, 1958), 482–483.

2. Vandana Shiva, *Stolen Harvest* (Lexington, KY: University Press of Kentucky, 2016): "Global corporations are not just stealing the harvest of farmers. They are stealing nature's harvest through genetic engineering and patents on life forms" (16).

3. World Health Organization, https://www.who.int › News › Fact sheets › Feb. 7, 2018.

4. Food and Agriculture Organization of the United Nations, "Gender Equity in Agriculture and Rural Development. A Quick Guide to Gender Mainstreaming in FAO's New Strategic Framework," 2009, ftp://ftp.fao.org/docrep/fao/012/i1240e/i12 40e00.pdf.

5. Ibid.: "Hidden behind complex free trade treaties are innovative ways to steal nature's harvest, the harvest of seed, and the harvest of nutrition."

6. Luce Irigaray, *The Sex Which Is Not One* (Ithaca, NY: Cornell University Press, 1985), 193. "Thus all economic organization is homosexual. . . . Women exist only as an occasion for mediation, transaction, transition, transference, between man and his fellow man, indeed between man and himself."

7. Mary Daly, *Gyn/Ecology* (Boston: Beacon Press, 1978), 9.

8. Judith Butler, *Antigone's Claim* (New York: Columbia University Press, 2000), 27–28. Contrasting the language of kinship with language of kingship, Butler states that Antigone's sin is that she speaks in the "language of sovereignty that is the instrument of political power," and that because she is female "her language is not that of a survivable political agency."

9. Mary Daly, *Gyn/Ecology*, 9 "Phallic myth and language generate legitimacy, and mask the material pollution that threatens to terminate all sentient life of this planet."

10. Luce Irigaray, *In the Beginning: She Was* (London; New York: Bloomsbury, 2013), 27. "In the beginning, the sage still listens to her—nature, Goddess, muse. They are the masters, for the philosopher who begins to speak. And his discourse still grows starting from the same depths as vegetal growth. It is not yet separated from them in order to constitute a logos parallel to a living world, which says this world while cutting it off from the roots of life and its becoming, transforming it into signs so as to put it to the disposal of the works of men . . . what is to be said, the philosopher then sets out on a path which is no longer that of wisdom but of arrogance of a demiurge" (27).

11. Erwin Schrodinger, *Nature and the Greeks* (Cambridge: Cambridge University Press, 1954), 25. "Parmenides' truth was the purest form of monism ever conceived."

12. G.S. Kirk, G.E. Raven, and M. Schofield, *The Presocratic Philosophers*, 2nd ed. (Cambridge: Cambridge University Press, 1983), 11. characterized the "archaic" as "naïve and irrational" (9–11). Joseph Owens, *History of Ancient Western Philosophy* (New York: Appleton Century Crofts, 1959), 11, describes the "archaic" as "the notion that the whole universe is animated and that the cosmic processes somehow parallel the vital activity of which men are conscious in their own living."

13. Robert Graves, *The White Goddess* (New York: Farrar, Straus and Giroux, 1948), 11. "Socrates, in turning his back on poetic myths, was really turning his back on the Moon-goddess who inspired them and who demanded that man should pay woman spiritual and sexual homage: what is called Platonic love, the philosopher's escape from the power of the Goddess into intellectual homosexuality, was really Socratic love."

14. Simone De Beauvoir, *The Second Sex* (New York: Vintage Books, 1974), xxiv. "Even when her rights are easily recognized in the abstract, long-standing custom prevents their full expression in the mores. In the economics sphere, men and women can be said to make up two castes; other things being equal, the former hold better jobs, get higher wages, and have more opportunity for advances than their competitors. In industry and politics, men have . . . more positions, and they monopolize the most important posts."

15. Food and Agriculture Organization of the United Nations, "Gender Equity in Agriculture and Rural Development. A Quick Guide to Gender Mainstreaming in FAO's New Strategic Framework," 2009, ftp://ftp.fao.org/docrep/fao/012/i1240e/i1240e00.pdf.

16. Rita Gross, *Buddhism after Patriarchy* (New York: State University of New York Press, 1993), 210. "Despite a strong basis in gender inequality in key Buddhist teachings, Buddhism's record on gender equality is not significantly better than any other religion."

17. Simone De Beauvoir, *The Second Sex*, xix "She is defined and differentiated with reference to man and not he with reference to her, she is incidental, the inessential as opposed to the essential. He is subject the Absolute-she is the Other."

18. Ibid., xxii–xxiii "Now, woman has always been man's dependent, if not his slave; the two sexes have never shared the world in equality. And even today, woman is heavily handicapped, though her situation is beginning to change. Almost nowhere is her legal status the same as man's and frequently it is much to her disadvantage."

19. Rosemary Radford Ruether, *Integrating Ecofeminism Globalization and World Religions* (New York: Roman and Littlefield, 2005), 124. "Dominology" is a "destructive impact on the environment by use of top-down epistemology and a concept of self and its relation to other humans and nature, is widely seen as the root of the evils of sexism, racism, imperialism, with its ongoing expression in neocolonial exploitation of third world societies and their natural resources."

20. Mary Daly, *Gyn/Ecology*, 29.

21. Rita Gross, *Buddhism after Patriarchy*, 141. "To a greater or lesser degree, most religions include a complex code of behavior considered to be divinely revealed or cosmically given that regulates daily life, including gender relationships."

22. Rosemary Radford Ruether, *Sexism and God Talk* (Boston: Beacon Press, 1983), 163.

23. Mary Daly, *Beyond God the Father* (Boston: Beacon Press, 1985), 163. "The dichotomizing-reifying-projecting syndrome has been characteristic of patriarchal consciousness."

24. Rosemary Radford Ruether, *Gaia and God* (New York: Harper and Collins Publishers, 1992), 247. "Eco-feminist theology and spirituality has tended to assume that the goddess we need for eco-logical well-being is the reverse of the God we have in Semitic monotheistic traditions."

25. Luce Irigaray, *The Sex Which Is Not One*, 86. "This model is always a *phallic* one, shares the values promulgated by patriarchal society and culture, values inscribed in the philosophical corpus: property, production, order, form unity, visibility . . . and erection."

26. Mary Daly, *Gyn/Ecology*, 13. "Indeed the texts of phallocratic ethicists function in the same manner as pornography, legitimating the institutions that degrade women's be-ing."

27. Ibid., 7. "I have coined the term *metapatriarchal* to describe the journey, because the prefix *meta* has multiple meanings. It incorporates the idea of 'post-patriarchal,' for it means occurring latter. It puts patriarchy in the past without denying that its walls/ruins and demons are still around. Since *meta* also means 'situated behind,' it suggests that the direction of the journey is into the Background. Another meaning of this prefix is 'change in, transformation of.' This, of course, suggests the transforming power of the journey. By this I do not mean that women's movement 'reforms' patriarchy, but that it transforms our Selves. Since *meta* means 'beyond, transcending,' it contains a built-in corrective to reductive notions of mere reformism."

Chapter 3

An Ecofeminist Response

As Audre Lorde has wittingly said, "the master's tools will never destroy the master's house."[1] This chapter focuses on outlining a practical and effective response to our ecological crisis without the "tools" of patriarchy. Counterbalancing problems such as land ownership, loss of biodiversity, globalization, poverty, and pollution without recourse to discourse or access to structures of power requires an epistemological shift beyond patriarchal conceptions and conventions. Indeed, many ecofeminists and social activists around the world are attempting to proceed along these lines. I will highlight some of their challenges and argue how and why the ecofeminist movement has failed to provide an adequate response.

The term "ecofeminism" was first used by Francoise d'Eaubonne in 1974 in her book *Le Feminisme ou la mort* to describe women's potential to bring about an ecological revolution.[2] Since then, the ecofeminism movement has evolved into a plurality of perspectives with the core belief in the interconnection between all living beings and the environment. There are important connections to be drawn between how women, minorities, and underprivileged classes are treated and, on the other hand, how the nonhuman environment, including animals and plants, is treated by patriarchy. In its very name, ecofeminism, a combination of two terms, shows itself to be intersectional. Ecofeminism has its roots in both the feminist movement and deep ecology, and it affirms the (historical, religious, political, empirical, epistemological, and metaphysical) connections between women and nature.

Examining and critiquing the connection between the domination of woman and nature has long been a cornerstone of the feminist movement. One of its goals is the eradication of gender-oppressive categories and the creation of a world where difference does not breed domination. The ecofeminist movement transforms the concerns of women as "other" into a larger context to include the nonhuman and the natural environment as well. Moving beyond traditional ethical theories, ecofeminism also informs and challenges the environmental movement by claiming that any adequate environmental ethics must include the interests of women and underrepresented peoples. Ecofeminism offers insights into both the feminist and ecological movements, affirming a multicultural analysis of the women-nature connection among all systems of domination and across all cultural/national lines. Standing against male-gender bias, ecofeminism seeks to develop and implement practices, policies, and theories that are holistic and life-affirming.

The intersectionality of ecofeminism is very clearly described by Karen Fox in "Leisure, Celebration and Resistance in the Ecofeminist Quilt," where she compares ecofeminism to a quilt comprised by the perspectives of women from all different backgrounds unified through the idea that the lives of women and the ecological condition are connected.[3] The problems that ecofeminism seeks to solve are one of the interlocking systems of domination. There is the problem of globalization with its colonial roots and its use of institutions like the World Bank, through which it has reinforced, upheld, and created divisions between the rich and the poor. It has choked out the economies of developing nations and allowed corporations to run rampant through those nations. It has allowed for the domination of environmental resources by a few people. It has allowed for the commodification of all things, including seeds, which has caused the destruction of biodiversity, and water, which has been contaminated by agricultural runoff and from other big businesses to the point that clean water is a commodity for elitist and privileged peoples. The former example illustrates how one problem is actually many. These many issues weave together to form an oppressive system that endangers nature and women. So in contemporary culture, any environmental ethics that does not take feminist concerns into account is alienating, and any feminist movement that is not environmental will fail.

All the problems presented by ecofeminism naturally lead to the question of what can be done. In many social justice circles, there are continual discussions regarding how bad things have gotten and how oppression and the marginalization of people need to end, but very rarely is there an overarching plan. Immediate action is extremely important, not just for social movements in general but also and especially for ecofeminism. This urgency is due to the immediacy of the destruction that neglecting the environment will cause, as well as the sheer magnitude of the devastation that all living beings will start experiencing. A movement cannot just be against something; it must also be *for* something. There must be an alternative toward which people are striving, even if that alternative would be brand new and hard to imagine presently.

The action needed in order to tackle the problems of interlocking systems of domination is twofold, both external and internal. In addressing an interconnected and intersectional web of problems, the ecofeminist movement offers a double-prong attack against ecological and social injustices. Some ecofeminists focus as well on the internal solution by issuing a call for a higher spiritual understanding of who we are and our relationships within the world.

Externally, we must revolt against all forms of oppression and domination. We must take action through social movements, grassroots organizations, protests, etc. A key component of any movement is having a clarity of mission. Another component to look at regarding these movements is durability and the ability to relate to a variety of concerns from different groups. So what does this mean for ecofeminism? It means that the place to start today as an individual to support the cause of ecofeminism is to talk to others about it. According to research by Erica Chenoweth, "for a peaceful mass movement to succeed, a maximum of 3.5% of the population needs to mobilize."[4] It is the job of those with information to spread it to those who do not have that information. This is something that is effective and that one can do right now. Recycling and cutting out meat in one's diet or planting a personal garden are important ways to connect with one's own natural environment and reduce one's carbon footprint. However, individual, solitary efforts are not what move social change along. The problems that are facing us are massive. There must be action and that action must be collective, so the first thing to do is to form that collective. But social activists alone will not change the way people think and interact on a daily basis; for that, we need a radical transformation and a consensus.

There seem to be three major problems embedded and entwined within the ecofeminist movement that impede momentum toward revolutionary social change. First and foremost is the issue of ethics itself, which traditionally is by male design in all prevailing cultures. No wonder most feminist and ecofeminist thinkers are reluctant to embrace a cohesive ethical theory. In addition to the fear of cultural imperialism, there is the concern over all of the other "isms" to which traditional ethical theory gives power. Naturally, ecofeminist thinkers would prefer to avoid the pitfalls of patriarchy. However, without some unifying vision, without a comprehensive approach, the ecofeminist movement lapses by failing to give credence to our very human need for a communal understanding of our collective being in the world. This is the very point of an ethics. So we must develop an ecofeminist ethics; otherwise, we remain with collection of more or less like-minded perspectives.

Second, in spite of the ecofeminist insistence on inclusivity, holism, and interconnection, ecofeminist approaches, for the most part, are plagued by the methods of patriarchy, namely, dualism. The reluctance to embrace a nondualistic philosophy is rooted in the concern over reduplicating the sins of the patriarchy. Either because of misconceptions of nondualism as some form of Western monism (with a homogenous transcendent idea of the one being removed from life) or due to the failure to grasp the dialectic nature of nondualism, Western ecofeminists seem mired in same methodological thinking as patriarchy.

Third, there is the question as to whether or not a spiritual component is necessary for the cause. One can embrace spirituality but certainly not impose it. In distinguishing between world religions and spirituality, admittedly world religions have done little to protect the environment and women. So ecofeminists are justified in being concerned. Moreover, regarding spirituality alone, apart from world religions, the fear of magical thinking raises its skeptical head. Yet, spirituality, like ethics, is vital for the integrity of the whole. Both provide a course of adjustment for relationships among beings in terms of conduct with one another and within the totality of being.

Before discussing any attempt at an ecofeminist ethics, we first need to examine what patriarchal ethical premises lead to condoning the mess we have made of our environment, nature, and all living beings in the first place. Traditional Western ethical theories rely on the notion of a rational self and on abstract principles. The concept of a rational self separates human beings from the rest of nature and perpetuates a dualistic discontinuity by failing to see humans as part of and continuous with nature. The domination of women by men and the domination of nature by humans both depend upon a particular logic. This logic of domination assumes and utilizes the premises that posit a difference of moral value between humans (with their rational moral agency) and the rest of nature. It asserts that the difference allows for humans to dominate nonhuman nature and for some humans to dominate other humans. This assertion reinforces the false assertion of male moral superiority and its pervasive dualistic imperialism.[5]

Today, many feminists, ecofeminists, and environmentalists are attempting to construct new paradigms for social justice and ecojustice.[6] In *Ecofeminist Philosophy,* Karen Warren lays out the eight-fold criteria for what she believes comprises an ecofeminist ethics. The first condition she describes is one of coherence, so that, though the theory is general and originates in a historical and conceptual setting, it is capable of evolving over time and as circumstances dictate. Second, she maintains that no feminist ethics should participate in any form of domination and shall oppose "any 'ism' that presupposes or advances a logic of domination." Third, it must be contextual and allow for a plurality of voices to emerge from other settings. Fourth, it must be inclusive. Fifth, no feminist ethic should lay claim to objectivity. Sixth, it must promote underrepresented values that have been dismissed or misrepresented in traditional ethical theory. Seventh and eighth, an ecofeminist ethics must reconceptualize what it means to be a human being making ethical choices, as well as the role, purpose, and limits of reason itself.[7]

Whereas Warren's approach provides us with a set of guidelines based on inclusion and growing coherence, it shies away from addressing the central problem of dualism head on. Any ecofeminist ethical theory must begin with the elimination of the category of "other." I would like to stress that we cannot eradicate the category of "other" unless we eradicate dualism. Once we stop envisioning ourselves as autonomous ethical agents wielding choices that divide and conquer, we can begin to see that what binds us together does not itself have or make distinctions. Nature is nature. It is not more here and less there, it is not separated from itself, so that one part is more valuable than other. It is whole. Thinking in terms of part to whole, rather than self and other, allows for an integrated experience of interconnection.

For many ecofeminist thinkers, social transformation cannot come about without radicalizing ourselves . . . and our thinking. In her groundbreaking *Gyn/Ecology,* Mary Daly issues a call, not for "female Self-sacrifice in male-led cause of 'ecology,'" but rather for women to discover/create/become part of the weaving process of a new beginning. Women's energies, what Daly calls "gynergy," help connect humans to each other and all that is and are contagious. The point is for women to break the codes of patriarchy and release the "Spring of be-ing."[8] For Daly, we step into a new space by casting off the role of "other," "which is the nothingness imposed by a sexist world."[9] In this light, I would emphasize that dualism itself allows for the splintering of our reality from being. As Daly says in *Pure Lust,* "there is, first of all the problem of dualism . . . Yet dualism, however subtle, is recognized as inadequate by Nag-Gnostic critics, for Naming the Reality of our Selves."[10]

In spite of the destructiveness of dualism, it keeps its stronghold on all prevalent modes of thought. Women in particular are suffering from a sort of "Stockholm syndrome" caused by patriarchy and its accompanying dualism. Invoking a nondualistic mindset requires that we change our fundamental premises about the nature of reality. In her article "Radical Nonduality in Ecofeminist Philosophy," Charlene Spretnak recognizes that there are several obstacles preventing Western society from adopting a radical non-dualistic philosophy. She maintains first that the postmodern scientific and objectivist epistemology is dismissive of anything that cannot be quantified. Subjectivity is considered an inferior form of knowledge because it cannot be measured. Likewise, nondual philosophies and spiritualities are rejected as simply magical thinking. As a second reason for the west's reluctance to embrace nondualism, Spretnak refers to the grip of deconstructive post-modernism on intellectual thought, particularly in academy, in seeing all concepts as social constructs. Third, she claims that feminists are skeptical of nondualism because of patriarchal interpretations and misrepresentations. Citing the duality of the category of "other" as a tendency of thought, she calls for an interpretation of nonduality as "a dynamic system of relations wherein any particular manifestation functions simultaneously as a distinct part and an unbroken whole."[11] Along with Spretnak's call, I would add that nondualism as a radical mindset eliminates bifurcated and divisive thinking of part against part, replacing it with thinking in terms of parts within a greater whole.

Furthermore, adopting a nondual approach solves a number of philosophical disputes and breaks the dichotomizing of conflicting narratives. First and foremost, it removes the false dilemma of the essentialist and deconstructionist debate. In a nondual framework either/or perspectives are reframed as conditions within a whole continuum rather than determinate limitations. We are conditioned by nature, conditioned by our environment, conditioned by an entire causal matrix of factors, including, and most especially, our psychosomatic selves. In analyzing notions of the self, Warren attempts to straddle the positions by claiming that there is a difference between conceptual essentialism and strategic essentialism. Rejecting conceptual essentialism as universalizing a set of properties, she defends a version of ecofeminism as strategic essentialism. Warren states that this view:

> permits, as a practical strategy, talk about commonalities, among individuals and groups as moral persons, selves, women and nature without thereby implying any biologically determined, socially unconstructed, conceptually essentialist account of moral persons, selves, women and nature.[12]

Of course, Warren is correct, we need a way of speaking in commonalities without alienating. However, while I appreciate that Warren is defending an ecofeminist philosophy, which she describes as "transformative," her distinction between conceptual and strategic essentialism adds yet another layer of dubious duality.

I contend that a full deconstruction of the dominant dualistic narrative has not been done, especially in terms of philosophical and political discourses. Jennifer Crawford, in promoting a nondual ecological self in relation to nature, challenges Valerie Plumwood's rejection of a nondual self. Crawford argues that "the non-dual approach, precisely by tackling dualism *per se,* may be just what is needed in the contemporary situation where multiple forms of oppression operate systematically across the boundaries of multiple dualism."[13] In order to see our way clear of competing tensions of opposites, nondualism encourages a complete deconstruction of the categories of self and other and thereby allows for a holistic and evolving understanding of self, self and nature, self in relation, and self as moral agent.

Nondualism is a cohesive and compressive set of premises (both epistemological and metaphysical) that ground us in the collective wholeness of "Be-ing."

Reconnecting with the oneness of nature/universe is not simply a matter for the mystic. Our experience of connection with what is, with "Be-ing," emanates from our interiority, but it must resonate outwardly to have any meaningful effect. Both the interior and the exterior, the inner and the outer, the internal and external are part of the organic whole of our selves. Nondualistic thinking does not view reality as abiding in a polarity of opposites but in harmony with the all-inclusive All. Nondualistic thinking calls for a necessary conversion of principles, both ethical and spiritual. This is an arduous journey, which many are reluctant to undertake.

Some ecofeminists do not see the need to include a spiritual component to the process of liberation for women and nature. In *Integrating Ecofeminism Globalization and World Religions,* Rosemary Radford Ruether discusses the tension between world religions and the environment. Radford Ruether acknowledges the role world religions play in alienating others and nature, but argues that religion is a "key component" in shaping moral value and "healing the anti-ecological worldviews of the past."[14] However, I would argue that world religions have exasperated the global situation and environmental crisis, and they continue to support the status quo of women and nature.

Furthermore, I propose that the distinction between religion and spirituality is crucial. According to Warren, the distinctions and opposing viewpoints concerning the role of spirituality in ecofeminism rest on the distinction between philosophy of religion and spirituality. Acknowledging this problem as justifiable, she nevertheless argues for the importance of ecofeminist spirituality "to intervene in and creatively change patriarchal (and other) systems of oppression."[15] Here I would argue that all world religions are man-made patriarchal institutions, therefore, suspect, and perhaps best avoided all together. Spirituality, on the other hand, as something apart from doctrine is a living presence in a person's life and cannot be superimposed from without.

While I believe that a spiritual attitude is necessary in framing the ecofeminist movement, I would add that we must be leery of the conceptual traps of essentialism, universalism, and imperialism. Spiritual experiences and developments may have shared characteristics, but spirituality is not a "one size fits all" type of thing. We must allow for a multiplicity of cultural models, meanings, and metaphors, as well as personal nuances. This would help to form an interwoven web of shared experiences instead of a codified dogma.

Depicting one model for spirituality, Warren, reminiscent of Kierkegaard, refers to spirituality as a "leap of faith." She describes spirituality as a person standing between two doors, one to the future that is in front of the person and one to the past or to what is familiar behind the person. This person is holding on to one door and trying to reach the other without letting go, but they cannot reach the door to the future and still hold onto the past, so they must let go. If they let go, there will be a moment wherein they will be suspended between each door, attached to neither. This suspension is what Warren means by spirituality or a "spiritual movement." What makes this movement spiritual is the acknowledgment of a belief in something other than oneself or, in addition to oneself, being able to sustain one when one is suspended.[16] In my view, Warren's model encourages a dynamic view of spirituality. Rather than seeing it as a fixed state or something to attain, the metaphor of leaping conjures a sense of impetus, of internal/eternal process of energy in motion.

Ecofeminist spiritualities in particular build upon the internal/eternal motion of spirituality. They are feminists in their commitment to ending patriarchy. They are spiritualities in their belief in life-affirming powers other than and in addition to oneself. Their ecofeminist focus is reflected in the intersectional commitment to care-sensitive practices directed at humans and the earth. Warren claims that at the core of this spirituality is a

> movement toward healthy, life-enhancing, nourishing, restorative values, beliefs, practices, and systems. This spirituality embodies power, one of much significance to individual well-being is "power-within power," which describes a mobilization of one's inner resources in order to survive.[17]

I believe that this internal aspect of the ecofeminist movement is addressed through a reworking of the self toward a higher, more intimate spiritual understanding of our relationships and roles within the world.

The central question of spirituality as a necessary component for the eco-feminist movement is: What does one mean by engaging in "spirituality" without defining, reifying, institutionalizing, and objectifying spirituality, as world religions tend to do. Ecofeminist spiritualities offer different paths and practices that reinforce our interconnections and relationships to nature, and they help develop our capacity for compassion by expanding our experiences and perspectives. This is not however, a completely subjective process because it involves concrete objective action. We must reinforce the connections between individuals and their environment as well as between each other.

One way in which systems of domination operate is by separating human beings from the environment. This false dualistic action allows for the destruction of nature to continue without care for the larger whole because one does not think the destruction of the environment directly involves oneself as part of it. This removal of the human being's intimacy with nature has damaging effects on the psyche. Spirituality practices can restore this intimacy by cultivating compassion. In this manner, we enter into a more meaningful communion with others like and unlike us, which is fortifying and life-affirming. Spirituality practices also grant us the ability to heal oppressive systems in a meaningful way that is for the good of all. The inter-locking systems of domination are oppressive, so the first thing required is to be able to survive long enough to change it. This is how spirituality becomes an important component of what one can do internally, that is, to use it as a fortifying agent in order to help us endure for the sake of all life on this planet. We survive as a community of beings or none of us survive. In this sense, not only is the personal the political, it is also the spiritual.

There are other ways to engage in spirituality. Mindfulness is one way. In this spiritual practice, individuals stay in the present, living completely in the moment, which is like being suspended in between the two doors that Warren depicts.[18] The notion of mindfulness is present in all religious traditions and all nature-based spiritualities. Although the practices themselves may differ, it is the same cultivation of awareness at the core. This awareness takes us out of ourselves as separate beings and places us in the midst of an open universe, as part of something greater than ourselves. It gives us that "something more," moving us from the ordinary to the extraordinary in our everyday lives. Whether we practice mindfulness through mediation, contemplation, or prayer, we learn to develop a sense of wholeness and connection. This sense is not idea, a tenet, doctrine, or theory, and it cannot be faked. It is a lived experience of authentic existence, mindfully aware that we all share the same ground of being. As the Buddhists might say, we need to bring mindfulness into action.[19]

One crucial aspect of spirituality is practice itself. Practice brings theory into action. It also enables us to unite body and mind. We cannot think ourselves into wholeness. We can think about baking a cake, but that is not the same as actually baking a cake. For spirituality to come into fruition, it must be embodied in and through action until it becomes habit and from that, if Aristotle is to be believed, a characteristic or state of our existence. Most religious traditions and forms of spirituality provide their followers with a "way" or "path" of conduct designed to concretize their teachings into an existentially lived reality that will enable the practitioner to develop spiritually. Without practice, whether it be prayer, mediation, contemplation, or any other form of dedicated action, spirituality would be empty thought and mere emotion.

Another way in which one could engage in spirituality is through a releasing of past notions and thinking patterns that have been used against us by patriarchy. As Daly maintains, patriarchy is not only a system in which people are suppressed by overt powers, it is also a system that has taken root within. The reworking of past notions, which Daly characterizes as a "spinning out," can be a way to engage spiritually within oneself. This way, we can combat oppressive mindsets that may have taken hold within us and subconsciously internalized as facts. For Daly, spirituality occurs when women exorcise the idea of "god the father" imbedded in their consciousness. In derarifying god, we became free from the fixed transcendent male god and freed into the fullness of our own being. According to Daly, "the problem is one of transforming the collective imagination so that this distortion of the human aspiration to transcendence loses its credibility."[20] By spinning into the fullness of being, we recognize that the Supreme Being is not a fixed entity but an intransitive verb, Be-ing, without an "other."

At some point, we must let go and allow ourselves to spin out of duality into wholeness. Indeed, many ecofeminist activists are proceeding accordingly. As a result, awareness is forming in our collective consciousness about our ecological fate and the fate of the planet. In my view, Vandana Shiva is a model among the many ecofeminist activists engaging in this process. Her holistic approach leads to ecological and human-rights activism by demanding responsibility from governmental and corporate entities. Shiva's work goes beyond educating us on the loss of biological and cultural diversity caused by political and private practices and policies. By employing the powerful kinetic aspects of the goddess, she clearly illustrates the legacy of the *Maya-Shakti-Devi* principle at work in the ecofeminist movement and advocates for ecojustice. Shiva draws particular attention to destructive ecological practices, such as the silencing of indigenous knowledge and the use of bioengineered seeds and agricultural products, such as pesticides. Engaged in the process of reclaiming nature and our spiritual consciousness, Shiva maintains that "what man does to the web of life, he does to himself."[21] Her message includes a reminder that Nature is the inventor, that She holds the trump cards over all patents, and that the loss of biodiversity caused by mankind's attempt at reigning in Her force will be countered by an equally destructive response. If we do not heed the reality of nature as primary, then the earth and all its living creatures will be destined to be put on life-support. Earth/Nature is alive, and in pain, and she cannot endure the abuse any longer. This is a call to act and to act mindfully. But what does one do on an ordinary Tuesday afternoon to create change?

I view writer and ecofeminist, StarHawk as a foremost example of ecospiritual activism in the West. She is a prime mover for earth-based spiritualities and neopaganism. Her unique approach synthesizes not just theory and practice but also everyday mindfulness, social and spiritual activism, faith and ritual. As an agent for change, she uses ritual as a grounding and galvanizing source/force for social justice. For StarHawk, ritual is a powerful tool for social change. She has organized numerous and effective ritual events not only as protests but also to change the energy of a situation, as a transformational act. In her breakthrough work, *The Spiral Dance,* she lays the basis for modern-day goddess worship. StarHawk states that the "feminist movement is a magico-spiritual movement as well as a political one."[22] Maintaining that energy moves in cycles transforming both the inner and outer worlds, she calls upon us to have to have inner and outer courage, to reacquaint ourselves with the goddesses of ancient myths and cultures, to create new ways of relating to each other and the earth, and to embrace the natural world so that we all may help heal from the ruptures of dualism.[23] In her book *Earth Path,* StarHawk offers a "corrective" reminder that we are "not *separate* from nature but in fact *are* nature."[24] For StarHawk, the earth is a living entity. On this point I propose that when we pay attention to this living earth and open ourselves to the rhythms of nature, we can learn to recognize that we live on common ground, in a common community.

When Lorde declared, "the master's tools will never destroy the master's house," she was calling for new tools, new methods, and new ways of thinking that move us out of patriarchal power struggles. StarHawk argues that change usually occurs from the edge and that one way to "change a system is to confront it with a different system,"[25] and she does. For StarHawk, as for many ecofeminists, including Warren, the paradigm of power as "power over" needs to be transformed into an understanding of power from within, and as a reminder that we are powerful together. StarHawk's insight is that the work for spiritual, ecological, and social justice cannot come about out of mere duty or through superimposed moral law codes, but instead is best undertaken freely out of true compassion. Recycling our trash out of duty is good, but when we act from a sense of care for the earth and for others, we give that same act an intentional energetic charge. This is the beauty of mind/body acting as one. This is the beauty of ritual as a conscious intentional act to create change.[26]

I believe it is important to realize that ritual need not be formularized or scripted, although it is usually conceived that way. Some will criticize this as magical thinking; in fact, it is energetic thinking. This is a mode of thinking in terms of energy and patterns, of thinking holistically, with balance, rather than dualistically in terms of opposing forces. Energy is what moves us. Synthesizing and reconciling ourselves with each other, with the earth, and with body/mind/heart creates a momentum that flows well beyond us. Starting from within and moving outward, aligning ourselves with new energy is the most radical ecologically and spiritually minded action that we can take.

The solutions for affirming social justice and healing our planet are not fast and easy. Nor can the task be done alone. First, women must free themselves from what Daly calls the "internalized patriarchal presence." Second, all humans need to strive for balance within a greater whole. Women especially need to bond together, to tell their stories and validate each other's narratives. As Daly claims, sisterhood is a powerful revolutionary action "that signals revolt and is itself the beginning of liberation."[27] Sisterhood is necessary for overcoming the side effects of religious-patriarchal constraints that have paralyzed women and contributed to global destruction. While dedicated and talented women strive for social change and ecological justice, countless more continue to support the shackles of their own oppression. Without a unifying worldview or spiritual perspective, the majority of women will still be inclined to identify with the religious and cultural values that have led to divergence, domination, and destruction. Without a comprehensive ethics that can sustain our planet, the unspeakable horrors to the earth and its many life forms will continue to predominate. Without enlightened cooperation among women, informed leadership falls to male domination.

Ethical theories created by patriarchy fail to recognize that the ground on which we stand is a living interconnected web of relations. Indeed, many recent and not so recent advances in quantum mechanics and unified field theory are proving this to be true. On a subatomic level, matter does not really exist as such but is instead a series of forces and relationships of interconnections and weavings, and maybe even intentionality.[28] The universe is a complex web of living relationships where life is sustained by and through those relationships. Reality, then, and by extension, morality is based on relationships. Life is created by relationships, and our lives, if we are to survive, must necessarily reflect that reality . . . morally.

What will it take for women to realize/own the force of their own energy? The need for women to take action is an existential moral choice about what type of world we want to live in. Spinning past patriarchal paradigms, we can weave patterns of thinking and values that are life-affirming and in keeping with sense of the sacredness of life. This is no ordinary leap of faith, indeed; it is a quantum leap . . . or as Daly called it a "hopping hope." If electrons can quantum leap then, so can we. We live in a universe of infinite possibility, where free radicals spin beyond their orbits to create change. Imagine a world with women quantum-leaping everywhere, free radicals, crossing time, space, institutions, bodies of knowledge and disciplines, disrupting the status quo, going beyond national, religious, and cultural man-made boundaries, coming together, not only to demand justice but to bring it. This is where a biophilic ethics begins, with a love for life . . . in all its forms. The time is now for women to reclaim their inherent sanity and safeguard the sanctity of life and justice in the universe, on the earth, in the home, village, and community. It is time to return to the earth and for that, we need a living ethos.

If be-ing is alive, then so is justice, which is the cornerstone of all ethics. A living ethics does not come from superimposed theories and rules of conduct but is instead an embodied justice originating from a biophilic sentience of the universe. Historically speaking, in the ancient movement from mythos to logos, from myth to reason, which traditionally designates the rise of classical philosophy, the vitality of justice gets lost. In order to overcome patriarchal and rudimentary notions of justice and provide a comprehensive living ethos for the ecofeminist movement, we need to go back and reclaim what was lost and stolen by patriarchy in its so-called rise of reason. A living ethos is biophilic and begins, not with abstract rational principles but with concrete relations. A biophilic ethic takes us back to basics, back to nature, back to each other, back to the relationship of the elementals, to the planets, to the stars and galaxies, and to this living earth. We do not exist in isolation from all that is. Thus, the primary motivation for a biophilic ethic is compassion and awareness of the interconnections between all beings and our codependence with nature. A biophilic understanding of the universe recognizes the dynamic emergence of justice as a living force inherent in the cosmos and reverberating through all our lives. In a biophilic ethic, justice, like the universe, is alive, and as we shall see in the next chapter, this is where we need to begin, once again.

NOTES

1. Audrey Lorde, "The Master's Tools Will Never Destroy the Master's House" in *This Bridge Called My Back Writings By Radical Women of Color*, eds. Cherrie Moraga and Gloria Anzaldua (New York: Kitchen Table Press, 1981), 98–101.

2. Mary Daly, *Gyn/Ecology* (Boston: Beacon Press, 1978), 9.

3. Karen Fox, "Leisure, Celebration and Resistance in the Ecofeminist Quilt" in *Ecofeminism*, ed. Karen Warren (Bloomington and Indianapolis: Indiana University Press, 1997), 155–175.

4. George Monbiot, "Only Rebellion Will Prevent an Ecological Apocalypse" in *The Guardian*, Guardian News and Media, 15 April 2019, www.theguardian.com/commentisfree/2019/apr/15/rebellion-prevent-ecological-apocalypse-civil-disobedience.

5. Karen J. Warren, *Ecofeminist Philosophy: A Western Perspective on What It Is and Why It Matters* (Lanham: Rowman & Littlefield, 2000), 23. "Some eco-feminist philosophers like Val Plumwood argue that the historical roots of the unjustified domination of nature originated in classical Greek philosophy and the rationalist tradition. For Plumwood, the culprit is 'rationalism,' the long-standing philosophical tradition that both defines rationality as the hallmark of humanness and elevates humans over non-human animals and nature grounds of human superior abilities to reason. Plumwood argues that human/nature value dualism at the heart of rationalism has spawned other harmful value dualisms (e.g., masculine/feminine, reason/emotion, spirit/body) . . . Plumwood criticizes environmental philosophy generally for its failure 'to engage properly various positions within the rationalistic tradition, which has been inimical to both women and nature.'"

6. Rosemary Radford Ruether, *Gaia and God* (New York: Harper and Collins Publishers, 1992), 3–4. "If dominating and destructive relations to the earth are interrelated with gender, class and racial domination, then a healed relation to the earth

cannot come about simply through technological 'fixes.' . . . In short it means we must speak of eco-justice, and not simply of domination of the earth as though that happened unrelated to social domination."

7. Warren, *Ecofeminist Philosophy: A Western Perspective on What It Is and Why It Matters*, 99–101.

8. Daly, *Gyn/Ecology*, 21.

9. Ibid., 41.

10. Mary Daly, *Pure Lust* (San Francisco: HarperSanFrancisco, 1984), 349.

11. Charlene Spretnak, "Radical Nonduality in Ecofeminist Philosophy," in *EcoFeminism, Women Culture and Nature*, ed. Karren Warren (Bloomington and Indianapolis: Indiana University Press, 1997), 425–436.

12. Warren, *Ecofeminist Philosophy: A Western Perspective on What It Is and Why It Matters*, 91.

13. Jennifer Crawford, *Spiritually Engaged Knowledge* (Hampshire, England, Ashgate, 205), 91.

14. Rosemary Radford Ruether, *Integrating Eco-Feminism, Globalization and World Religions* (New York: Roman and Littlefield, 2005), 47.

15. Warren, *Ecofeminist Philosophy: A Western Perspective on What It Is and Why It Matters*, 193–195.

16. Ibid., 195–198.

17. Ibid.

18. Ibid., 193–195.

19. In addition to the Buddhists' many sophisticated meditation techniques, we have seen the rise of the movement for socially engaged Buddhism which contains environmental, spiritual, and social justice concerns. One of the primary leaders of this movement is Zen monk, Thich Nhat Hanh. See also David Chappell, ed. *Buddhist Peacework* (Boston, Wisdom Publications 1999).

20. Mary Daly, *Beyond God the Father* (Boston: Beacon Press, 1973), 19.

21. Vandana Shiva, *Stolen Harvest* (Kentucky: University Press of Kentucky, 2016), 74–75.

22. StarHawk, *The Spiral Dance* (San Francisco: HarperSanFrancisco, 1979), 208.

23. Ibid., 201.

24. StarHawk, *Earth Path* (New York: HarperOne, 2004), 9.

25. Ibid., 37.

26. Ibid., 6. "Our magical practices arose from people who were deeply connected to the natural world, and our rituals were designed to give back to the world, to help maintain its balance. If we leave the natural world out of our practice and rituals in any real sense, if we invoke an abstract earth but never have any real dirt under our fingernails, our spiritual, psychic, and physical health becomes devitalized and deeply imbalanced."

27. Daly, *Beyond God the Father*, 60.

28. The Dali Lama, Herbert Benson, Robert Thurman, Howard Gardner, Daniel Goldman and participants in the Harvard Mind Science Symposium, *Mind/Science Symposium: An East-West Dialogue* (Boston: Wisdom Publication, 1991).

Chapter 4

Reclaiming the Narrative: From Mythos to Ethos

This chapter examines the matriarchal traditions and goddess worship as preserved and illustrated in ancient myth. Re-envisioning discourse and narrative without the religious, political, and philosophical platform afforded by patriarchy has long led to the practice of reinterpretation. This practice is one of the great functions myth generally offers society: to be formed and reformed again while still preserving a commonality and set of principles, esoteric as they sometimes may be. Without the burden of cultural nuances and social protocols, ancient myth provides a core positive and proactive message that resonates with a heightened sense of justice and responsibility for the earth. Utilizing these mythical conceptions, this chapter will argue that such mythical conceptions reflect and demand a living ethos of embodied justice and holistic activism that stands in sharp contrast to our current patriarchal conceptions of justice, social practices, and international policies.

In spite of all of the work being done on ancient goddess religions, women and spirituality, and environmental ethics, patriarchy, and dualism still cloud any new momentum. While the awareness of ecological problems facing us is at an all-time high, political, religious, and cultural factors serve as impediments for change. As Daly has repeatedly claimed, women, including even feminists, have been "intimidated into Self-deception, becoming the only Self-described oppressed group who will not name their oppressor."[1] Naming, in this sense, is a liberating act, but if women refer to their oppressor only in vagaries and abstractions, then nothing will change. Daly further claims that it is males and males only who are the "originators, planners, controllers, and legitimators of patriarchy."[2] However, women can benefit from the social status afforded to them by certain patriarchal protections and power structures, causing them to internalize a male model. Moreover, patriarchy is not gender-limited, and its weapons of choice are not only sexism, classism, elitism, or imperialism but also, at its core, dualism.

In the west, we are told that the story of the universe begins with the Word, *logos*. However, logos is already an abstraction, a superimposition, and a rationalization against the primordial unity of the oneness of a living universe. Myths about this primordial universe can liberate us if we seek out their deeper meaning. As we learn from prehistory, our earliest prepatriarchal myths were centered on the Mother Goddess as the representative of a living universe. Reflecting the concerns of our ancient ancestors, these ancient myths were focused on nature and the continuous cycle of life, death, and rebirth, and they aimed to imbue the believer with a spiritual sense of the connectedness of being part of a greater whole in a sacred process.

Unfortunately, even our earliest myths of the great Mother Goddess have not been excluded from the takeover by patriarchy. The patriarchal Indo-European myths of the herding tribal communities, in contrast, invoke the symbolism of the father-God as the divine creator and originator of moral and social laws that have helped to maintain the patriarchal values of power and order. Dismissing the role of the Mother Goddess as divine creatrix and stripping her of her power, patriarchal myths have usurped the original meaning of ancient goddess myths, turning her truths of Nature into handmaidens of patriarchy. By violating the original meaning of the ancient goddess myths, patriarchal myths established patriarchal rule and set the standards for law and morality, creating a society where we all serve the "father." This serving in the name of the father turns the cycles of nature into vicious cycles of domination and oppression, resulting in social and ecological destruction.

Among the numerous examples of patriarchy appropriating/utilizing ancient goddess myth for its own purposes, the classical Greek myths contain two cultural themes: the dominant patriarchal culture of the Hellenes and the persistent agriculturally centered tradition of pre-Indo-European goddess worship. Archaic myths testify to the Aryan patriarchal culture's exploitations in suppressing the earlier goddess worship cult and the matriarchal elements of an indigenous tradition. The epics of Homer and Hesiod represent the tradition of a dominant culture of hierarchy, power, and warlike tendencies over and against matriarchal subculture, which existed in the temples and the fields of the people. This struggle culminated "when the *Iliad* was composed and kings boasted: 'We are far better than our fathers' (signaling the queen's) eclipse by an unlimited male monarchy."[3] Of course, the most notable symbolism in this struggle is the beheading of Medusa, which represents the slaying of the goddess by patriarchy. Medusa, portrayed as a Gorgon monster with snakes for hair who turned men to stone, was both feared and reviled. However, her role was that of the protectress who safeguards her mysteries and ensures that they are not violated by the uninitiated and profane. When

Perseus beheads Medusa, he represents the patriarchal culture of the Hellenes succeeding in conquering the power of the Goddess.[4]

Though not a goddess, the figure of Antigone in Greek culture speaks volumes to man's attempt to silence women and their power. Even if Antigone herself has been silenced and put to death, her defiant deed reminds women of our primordial strength. Sophocles's myth represents the quintessential feminist tragedy for women whose words and deeds are not understood, or perhaps, understood too well. By defying the king's rule of law and burying her brother, Antigone thwarts the sovereignty of patriarchy in favor of a higher order. By breaking the law ordained by the king, Antigone places herself out of the political and ethical sphere of discourse. Her defense is unintelligible, for she cannot justify her actions according to the laws and language of the king, so her words and deeds cannot be assimilated by the state. She stands outside of the predominant logos of patriarchy and can only claim a rule of law based on something other than patriarchy, namely kinship, or blood line, or matriarchy itself.[5] Hence, her challenge to Creon is unjustifiable and unforgivable. Perhaps Sophocles's intention is to remind women to keep their place and not to be guilty of hubris. No pre- or meta-patriarchal position or language is tolerated; in fact, such positions cannot even be spoken or heard. Women are silent because they stand outside the logos. Women will have to learn another language other than the discourse of patriarchy if they are to speak and be heard, even to themselves.

History and myth converge over and over again. From a religious-political perspective, most of Western history can be viewed as the repetition of the act of patriarchy over-powering the role of the Goddess. Yet, we still can hear the heart of the Goddess beating in many of the well-known patriarchal myths of world religions. By tracing back Her message, we can reclaim Her truths and transform Her back to life.

By beginning with myth, we move beyond the particular into the universal. Myth, by its nature is transformative. As Mircea Eliade points out, myth speaks of human activity as creative and exemplary, becoming a model for the whole world. In this sense, myth provides and constitutes a primitive spirituality that transcends dualities and reveals the mysteries.[6] Myth thereby extends itself beyond the merely rational and particular into the sacred and spiritual realms. Though myth may spring from particular cultures and historical contexts, it speaks to the growth of the human spirit by connecting us to the totality of what is and, thereby enabling the totality to become a reality. As Eliade states, "Before they became main philosophical concepts, the One, the Unity, the Totality were desires revealed in myth and proves that the mystery of totality forms and integral part of human drama."[7]

Without myth, we are left with the mundane, and the strangle of so-called rationality imposed upon human desire. Myth is a vehicle of transformation from the everyday secular consciousness to a primordial awareness of eternal models of the spiritual journey. It is never just a myth. All major religious traditions have at their core the goddess myth. Life, death, rebirth, the cycles of nature, the modes of consciousness, the unending revolutions of creation, the turning of the wheel, this is the dance of life, both as manifest and unmanifest.

The stories differ from culture to culture, but the meaning of the myth is the same. For example, in India, the goddesses *Maya*, *Shakti*, and *Deva* help form the Hindu pantheon of gods and goddesses representing the two aspects of creation. The Goddess Shakti is highly regarded as vital energy of life, the charge to existence, the unseen force that gives rise to the universe. In ancient Babylon, Innana descends into the underworld to save her lover Osiris from death and restore him to life. In Egypt, Isis too saves her lover Horus from having been ravaged to death by reconstituting him and restoring his vital powers. Just as the goddess on a cosmic level must descend into the underworld to reclaim energy and magically transform death to rebirth, so too must every woman descend into her own unconsciousness to find her authentic self and true powers. Thus, to embody the goddess myth is to undergo a revolution of consciousness.

In Eleusis initiation was confirmed through the power of the Great Mother herself. She is identified as the Goddess of grain, fertility, life, death, and rebirth. Demeter is the Earth Mother Goddess of Greek mythology, whose name itself is the root of the word "mother." According to tradition, she is the daughter of Cronus and Rhea. Together with her four daughters (Athena, Artemis, Psyche, and Persephone), they comprise the basis of the Goddesses of the Greek Parthenon. Throughout Greece, the mystery cults of Demeter were reenacted according to the same format and decree of the Goddess. The myth of Demeter is itself about resurrection and rebirth.

The story of Demeter is not a simple story about the changing of the seasons. It is a virtual Rosetta stone for women to claim their power. According to legend, Demeter, the Earth Mother, Goddess of grain, refused to allow anything to grow until her daughter Persephone was returned to her from the underworld. One day, while Persephone was with her sisters picking wild flowers, she was abducted by Hades, the god of the underworld. Demeter's grief was inconsolable. In her despair and rage, she wandered the face of the earth searching for her daughter. In order to discover her whereabouts, she sought solace at Eleusis on the top of a mountain spur overlooking the Aegean. Here, on Mount Eleusis she weeps for her lost daughter into the well of the earth, where she is given courage by the demi-goddess Baubo, whose name refers to belly or belly laugh.

Baubo is known for her fecundity and cosmic play. When she heard of Demeter's grief, she spread open her legs revealing her vulva to Demeter and laughing. This gesture was meant to remind Demeter of her powers as a goddess, that she is the source of creation and creativity, of the paradoxes of life and death.

When Demeter was reminded of her creative powers, she issued forth a decree for her order as Earth Mother was as sacred law. She vowed that nothing would grow unless and until Persephone was returned to her. This is the story of the changing of the seasons of life, death and rebirth. Because Persephone partook of food in the underworld, she could only return to earth for a period of six to eight months at which time, the earth gives forth Her abundance. Later, in winter, when the earth grows cold, Persephone returns to the underworld only to reemerge again in spring. Here, the Christian myth of the resurrection can be seen as based on the Goddess motif of descent and return.

For centuries, the process of descent and return was reenacted by Demeter's followers at Mt. Eleusis. These rituals/sacred rites were essentially initiation ceremonies that were known as the Eleusinian Mysteries. Women from all over the ancient world came to reenact these Mysteries rites twice a year in the spring and fall. These Mystery rites were sacred and secret, and participants were held to the highest standards of observance. The followers of Demeter's Mystery cults came together to celebrate the eternity of life, the cycle of creation, and the power of women.

The Eleusinian Mysteries conform to older Egyptian and Persian Mysteries representing the continuous process of descent, search, and ascent. Little is known of the actual rituals themselves, except that they are said to be transformative by nature. As part of the theme of the transformation of wheat, the symbol of sustenance and agriculture becomes embedded in the process, as does the drinking of the sacred potion. By descending into the underworld and searching the abyss, practitioners confront the unconsciousness process of life and death, and emerge to the plane of conscious life once again. The rituals were comprised of three parts: "things done" referring to the reenactment of the myth, "things shown," referring to sacred objects, and "things said," referring to orations and commentaries, and possibly chants or prayers

Initiation ceremonies were designed to have participants experience the original goddess myth. Much of the actual rituals were designed to empower the initiate, and they embodied the mythic path of the Goddess in accordance with the teachings. The lessons are a reminder for women to own their Goddess power. Originally understood, Goddess rituals were about the creative power of women, and the Goddess was seen as life-giver and redeemer who kept the turning of the wheel of the seasons and cycles of life and death.

The Christian myth of the resurrection, for example, can be seen as based on the Goddess motif of descent and return.

Another example of the goddess myth of life, death, and rebirth that corresponds to Demeter in the ancient world is found in the goddess-worshiping society in ancient Egypt. Known for their monolithic pyramids, writing system, artwork, and astrology, the ancient Egyptians worshipped a variety of Goddesses and Gods, many with some animal traits connecting them to women and the world of nature in general. One of the most important Goddesses was Isis, who represents the characteristics of healing, magic, and fertility. Here too, we find the creative powers of the life-giving Goddess overcoming death.

Isis is one of the oldest goddesses who was worshipped for centuries throughout the ancient world. Her cult spread from Egypt to Greece and the Roman world, where her temples were erected. She is still venerated today by modern-day pagans. Her name refers to throne and majesty, as she was said to have powers over life, death, and rebirth. She is the daughter of Geb, God of the earth, and Nut, Goddess of the sky. She married her bother Osiris. The details of the story vary in detail, but the meaning is the same. Osiris was tricked by Set into stepping into a wooden box that, unknowingly, for Osiris would become his coffin. Wanting to ensure Osiris's complete destruction, Set cut up Osiris's body into fourteen pieces and casted them about the earth. Isis, in her grief, set out to restore Osiris's body. She found thirteen parts of him, all but his phallus. She constructed a new phallus for him and, by her magical powers, restored him to life temporarily; at least, long enough for her to conceive a child, Horus, who would eventually become king. According to some, the depiction of Isis holding Horus to her breasts forms the basis of the image of the Madonna with the baby Jesus. After Horus's conception, Osiris returns to the underworld. Because of Isis's powers of life over death, she becomes the archetype of the Mother-Goddess, inspiring the role of women as mothers and magicians. As a role model for women, Isis is seen as the Queen of Heaven. Every year in the ancient world when the Nile flooded, festivals were held in her honor, as it was said that the Nile became filled with Isis's tears. Incorporating the attributes of the Mother Goddess Isis inspires women to recognize their power for creation, majesty, and love.

Originating in Mesopotamia, Inanna is one of the oldest Goddesses, dating back to 4,000 BCE. Her story too tells us of the pathways to creative power. She was worshipped throughout ancient Babylon and Sumer. Temples and shrines dedicated to her can be found up and down the Tigress and Euphrates Rivers. Her history, personality, and powers are not a little complicated. Traditions differ about her origins, but as the protectress of an agriculture people, her stories, myths, and hymns circulated for centuries throughout the regions. The lion is her symbol of power. Later, she becomes identified with her Akkadian counterpart, Ishtar. Myths and legends abound concerning her exploits. She is even mentioned in the story of Gilgamesh for her ill-treatment of her lovers. Never formally married, her exploits are many and varied, as she leaves a trail of broken hearts. As the goddess of both love and war, she is known for her sexual and political ambition.

It is said in one myth that Inanna sent her lover, Dumuzi, to the underworld, and later with the help of her minister, Nincubura, descends to the underworld herself to bring him back for six months every year. Her descent into the underworld and subsequent return symbolize the descent into the unconscious and return to a renewed awareness. As told in one of her hymns, "from the great heaven the goddess set her mind on the great below." Representing the cycle of eternal return, she is identified with the planet Venus, the morning, and evening stars. As Venus rises in the morning, sets in the evening and rises again, so the mythical movements of Inanna's descent duplicate the physical movements of the planet Venus. Inanna's journey represents every woman's process of descending to the depths of their own psyche to find their power.

The magic of life, death, and rebirth was the domain of the Goddess, and her ways were practiced throughout the worlds. Prior to Christianity, long before the male god, the mystery of creation was the exclusive power of female creativity. Following the Greeks, the Christians embarked upon the same mission of converting the myth to reality, converting pagans into Christians, and converting the primordial unity of goddess into the tensions of the Logos upon the world. As Robert Graves states: "This new God claimed to be dominant as pure Good, pure Logic, able to exit without the aid of women. This outcome was philosophical dualism with all the tragic-comic woes attendant on spiritual dichotomy."[8] What was really being waged was a conversion to a new world order, where the decrees of the Goddess become subsumed to man's word, to be replaced by man-made law. Patriarchal norms and religious institutions sought nothing short of the total obliteration of the old-world view of the Goddess being replaced by an entirely new ethical system.[9]

In Europe, not only were most of the Goddess temples destroyed and resurrected as churches, but Her symbols were transmuted into symbols of evil. The most obvious example is in the Old Testament, with the snake as the personification of evil. For centuries past, the snake had been the symbol of the goddess, presumably because of its resemblance to the umbilical cord. In the Asian traditions, it corresponds to the Kundalini at the base of the spine indicative of the sacred energies of the Goddess infusing the human spinal system. In these cases, the imagery was not lost on our ancestors who long sought to continue with their Mother Goddess worship traditions, in spite of the systematic and systemic feudal rule of the fathers.

Another instance of the wrenching of symbols from the Goddess found in *Genesis,* comes to us in the form of the vilifying of the apple, the proverbial forbidden fruit. Why the apple? Because no matter how innocuous the object, if it represents an aspect of the Goddess, it must be appropriated and made holy by the father, a "bait and switch" tactic that has proved effective. The apple, as innocent as it may now appear was a long-standing the symbol of the Goddess. As Robert Graves explains, "For if the apple is halved cross-wise each half shows a five-pointed star in the center, emblem of immortality, which represents the Goddess in her five stations from birth to death and back again.[10]

Finally, in a desperate attempt to capture the reluctant pagans, Christianity elevated the role of Mary or rather dethroned her as the Triple Goddess and cosmic mother and regulated her to the role of the unfortunate (and perhaps unwilling) receptacle of male authority. Mother of god, indeed! Gone is the queen of Heaven, and so much has been lost by such patriarchal perversions. Christianity was born, not by virtue of a son, but by death of the Mother. In fact, its entire foundation rests literally on the body of the Mother-Goddess. Daly, citing with approval Elizabeth Cady Stanton's claim that if one removes, "the snake, the fruit tree and women from the tableau, we have no fall, . . . no everlasting punishment—hence no need of a savior. Thus, the bottom falls out of the whole Christian theology."[11]

Even today, in India, where goddess worship is still practiced, we find social and political roles of feminine energy still under the sway of masculine forces, in spite of any spiritual claims to the contrary. The role of the Goddess was incorporated rather late into the elite Sanskrit tradition. In the early stages of the Hindu pantheon, the Goddess figured strongly in mythology, but not as a major deity. Usually, goddesses were portrayed as wives or consorts of the gods, but there was little emphasis on their cosmological or ontological significance. Eventually, Goddesses as individual deities began to emerge in Sanskrit literature in the Brahmanical tradition. Goddesses who were paired as consorts to the gods became instrumental in their partners' activities or even dominant over them. Moreover, there was a growing tendency to conceive of an independent cosmic goddess, *Devi*, or Great Goddess, *MahaDevi* who contains all goddesses within her. Eventually, a full-blown cult of the Mother-Goddess had formed and became the basis of the Shakti tradition.

Properly speaking, *Maya-Shakti-Devi*, or *MahaDevi* is not a single deity but, instead, represents many indigenous forms. Worship of the Goddess is part of the ancient Hindu/Vedic pantheon. *Devi*, or *MayaDevi* is the universal mother and the embodiment of the female energy of God. She is a manifestation of the supreme being. She is the Mother of all life energy, both the seen and the unseen, the conscious and unconscious. She restores cosmic order and, like the earth, absorbs all things into Herself. Her body is the universe itself, and beyond.

Mythically understood, the Great Mother Goddess, *MayaDevi*, generates all that is, and she is identified with the God *Vishnu's* second wife, the earth, or nature. She can appear in many forms in the natural world or as a living being, as wife, mother, young girl, or old woman. Some of her many representations include *Durga,* slayer of the buffalo demon, *Kali,* the warrior who personifies the wrath of women, and *Shakti,* the energy of the gods. One of the more known forms of the Great Mother Goddess is *Shakti*, the consort of *Shiva.* This male/female energy is the personification of the dynamic powers of being. The *Shakti* principle as feminine energy is what is essential to life. *Vishnu* dreams the dream of creation, but his power lies dormant. It requires female kinetic energy to awaken. Without female kinetic energy, there is no creation and no evolution of consciousness.

These representations tell us that *MayaDevi* is power, creativity, and the world-cycle itself. She encompasses light and sound, form and the formless, purity and impurity, the auspicious and the inauspicious, creation and destruction. Her nature is paradoxical. Manifest and unmanifest, She reveals and conceals reality and beyond, yet she is that self-same reality. This dual face of *MayaDevi* underscores her functions as both earth Mother-Goddess and cosmic principle. Yet this polarity is not the balance of opposites, but the all-encompassing reality of her pervasive oneness.

In Mahayana Buddhism, Kwan Yin is the Goddess of compassion and mercy. She originated in ancient India, and in the Sanskrit tradition was known as Avalokitesvara. Even though Avalokitesvara appeared in male form, his feminine qualities of compassion, mercy, and universal love eventually transformed into a female version that emerged in China in the first century as Kwan Yin, and later in Thailand and Japan. She is also said to be comparable to the Green Tara in Tibetan Buddhism. She is sometimes depicted as having many heads because one is not enough, and as having many arms to do all the work that must be done. She can appear in many forms across cultures, and she is worshipped throughout eastern Asia. She embodies the Buddhist goal of being a true Bodhisattva, and, as such, her nature is pure divine love and mercy. As a Bodhisattva, Kwan Yin's role is not merely to help alleviate human suffering, but also in taking the Bodhisattva vow, she chooses never to cross over to enlightenment until all beings have achieved freedom from suffering. She remains, life cycle after life cycle, in order to assist humans and all beings on the path of life, death, and rebirth. Having been sentenced to death by her father, she herself is said to have descended to the underworld by taking on the guilt of her executioner. Once in the underworld, she bore witness to all of the sufferings in the various stages of hell. Moved by great compassion, Kwan Yin harnesses all of her power and good karma to free many souls back to the world. Yama, the god of the underworld, is forced to send her back to earth, lest she destroy his underworld. Kwan Yin's presence is to remind us that true compassion transforms both ourselves and the world.

In Tibetan Buddhism, we encounter the "Mother of the Buddhas." Here the Great Mother is seen as essential emptiness, which is the basis for all identity and relation. Her presence refers to the feminine power of creativity and birth and, more specifically, as pure potentiality or empty space. As the Mother of creation, Her essential emptiness is the basic space that contains everything that is and gives birth to creation. Just as *Maya* is not mere illusion, the primordial Mother of Tantra Buddhism is not mere emptiness. As the womb, which is reality, she is the measure of all things and weaves the substance of events. Her creative powers make her the Mother of the dharmas. To Her belong, not only the gate of birth and creativity but also the gate of enlightenment.

The Great Mother Goddess's function in either Hinduism or Buddhism allows for a personal and spiritual healing that bridges the problems usually associated with the dichotomizing of spirit and matter, self and other, and the scared and profane. The role of *MayaDevi* is as both Earth Mother and cosmological principle. The predominant focus, however, tends toward notions of embodiment, creativity, and interconnection, with little emphasis placed on her ontological function as creatrix. Her presence, emerging out of patriarchal myth and construction links the goddess as the principle of creativity and cycles of creation to the female body, in terms of fertility and menstruation. Her symbolism and allotted role (along with all accompanying social ills and realities of gender inequality) can be critically viewed as a symptom of patriarchy's continual fixation on the female body with the dismissal of the Goddess's cosmological powers.

Worship of the Goddess as Earth Mother is different than worship of the Goddess as cosmogonic principle, which is the regulating force of the universe itself. As cosmogonic principle, the great Mother Goddess is beyond even the gods and as such, is no longer Hindu or Brahminical. She is beyond the dharmas, and beyond all religious conception. In the Hindu and Buddhist traditions, the great Mother Goddess appears in myth and is assigned form, but her cosmogenic nature is preserved truly in her formlessness, in her all-pervasive oneness/emptiness. A return to the Great Mother Goddess requires, not just a recognition of how She forms nature but also celebration of cosmogenic unity. The ancient myths of the great Mother Goddess, which celebrated her primordial formless nature, are hidden in the rituals and doctrines of the present. In Her original state, she is ontologically prior to all. She is the primordial one. She reinforces the fact that primordial nature is beyond all distinctions. By the many roles the Goddess takes in myth, it is appropriate to assume that She is the representative of be-ing as she who is both one and the all. Her presence can help us see through the veil of illusion, and this is perhaps what can alleviate our global obsession with patriarchal idolatry.

Plato's famous Allegory of the Cave is a notorious example of patriarchy idolatry. The imagery of the cave motif represents humanity's movement away from the womb of goddess worship and the unconscious into the light of patriarchal reason itself. This hyperactive tendency to structure everything according to the dictates of the male mind creates the static one-dimensional, one-sided logos for which there is no alternative discourse. Unless, of course, we take the goddess myth seriously as a living force of cosmological justice. Myth becomes alive when we embody its meaning. The logos does not eclipse primordial oneness. The goddess motif of life, death, and rebirth is energetically reenacted in every woman, whether we are aware of it or not. However, just as it is in the myth itself, when done consciously, women can become the ethical force of justice.

In the ancient gynocentric cultures, the message was clearly articulated that Justice is the way of Being. As an original manifestation of the Great Mother, her role was to stress the nonduality of what is. Her presence indicates that Justice is not seen as separate from reality or as imposition, but indeed as the necessary limit/measure of creativity, which not fragmented as part of a social construction, but as the whole embodiment of energy. This idea of justice runs through all the earliest manifestations of Indo-European prehistory and indigenous religions. Further, as we have seen in the first chapter, her role as Justice is to ensure the dynamic of be-ing, indeed in the unity which encompasses all opposites. Justice herself is beyond the duality of good and evil, and beyond that which is manifested and that which is concealed. As the embodiment of the creative principle, the Goddess's role as Justice is not only centered on existence but also mediates between that which is beyond existence and nonexistence, including pure potentiality. Justice is not a what but a who. It is the Goddess herself who binds the universe together.

In constructing an ecofeminist vision, the symbols and meanings of ancient goddess religions can help to focus on the principles of the great Mother-Goddess, so as to avoid perpetuating yet another false dichotomy of opposites. The great Mother Goddess is in principle beyond all opposites and dualities, containing them and balancing them within herself. She is the primordial oneness. Her presence indicates that we take the seeming duality of nature as a primordial unity, where Justice as such is not an abstraction from the whole but an intimate and harmonizing force within it. In this manner, the principles of ecofeminist spirituality afford a worldview invested in sustainability, cultivation of life, and wholeness. Ultimately, however, in all of the above, something essential is left out.

In reconstructing the role and symbols of the great Mother Goddess modern literature has tended to focus on her positive nature: wisdom, compassion, creation, and interconnection. The idea of the angry, the energetic aspect of the Goddess is still taboo, but what is missing in this aversion is the understanding of the role of the goddess as protectress. By embracing the great-Mother Goddess, we are not simply giving divinity a sex change, replacing one idolatrous image for another, but instead realigning and transforming into a new orbit of justice. The justice of the great Mother Goddess demands that we take the seeming duality of nature as primordial oneness. Her justice is not the mere retribution but the balance of opposites and the full expression of her all-pervasive oneness. In contrast to a patriarchal sense of justice based on human construct, laws and norms, the justice of the Goddess is based on the reality of nature, and harmonizing and preservation of the whole. Part of her triple function as the great goddess is that of the avenging force of nature, creation *and* destruction, good *and* evil, life *and* death. Her function of justice can be severe and horrific: this is the dark side of Justice.

The manifest action of Her justice in nature can be seen as a corrective/corelative response to destructive and imbalanced human activities: melting glaciers and polar ice caps, violent shifting weather patterns, raging fires, tsunamis and super viruses, are a few examples of Her response. This destructive response is not a punitive and abstract retribution for its own sake, but the necessary force of the totality of the whole maintaining cosmic order and ecological stability. In speaking of eco-justice, we step out of duality into the oneness of nature. Justice resides in its own orbit within the great Mother Goddess as a principle of energy; not dualistic but all encompassing, and unyieldingly aware of the interconnectedness of all that is.

In reclaiming and reconstructing ancient goddess myths, eco-feminists can move us beyond the present patriarchal discourses associated with power and hierarchy into a narrative which constructs an emerging ethos that is not dominated by abstract principles, but by living relationships. However, first, we need to remove the veil from our eyes and reclaim the original meaning of some of our most enduring mythical stories and see them from the perspective of the Goddess herself. In this way, we are not only telling a story but bringing the story to life, in our own bodies, in our own lives. As women learn to identify more and more with the Goddess, they learn to become the story.[12] Women become living Justice. This transforms everything.

Daly says that "women on our own Journey are discovering Metis and the third-born Athena: our new be-ing."[13] While the resurrection of the goddess myth helps empower us, it is only through our own descent and return into our recess of our psyches that we empower ourselves. We have endured in the man-made dumps and mind/mine fields of patriarchy long enough. The Goddess within is calling for a new ethos and a new way of be-ing, creating a radical rupture from the dead past into a living presence-ing.

The Goddess is rising, but will we recognize Her when we see Her? Recently, across the world, we have seen the women's movement mount protest after protest about everything from securing women's reproductive rights to equal pay to combating ecological destruction and climate change to social justice issues to the #metoo movement. These individual women show the face of the Goddess. In spite of the temptation for imagery and concretization, we do not need another archetype. The faces of the great Mother Goddess are too many and too varied to be contained in any one image or persona. She is Earth Mother, Cosmic Mother, Avenging Justice, and Warrior Goddess. She is a prostitute, a privileged academic, a mother of three, homeless, rich, poor, young old, black, white, yellow and brown, rural and urban, third world, new world, new age. She is the face of every woman. She is arising from within us, not from without, and her wisdom knows no boundaries. She will not be contained and she will not be violated any longer.

As we are in the age of Kali Yuga (the age of destruction), perhaps we should embrace it, or at least understand this type of destruction for what it is. As I write this, the Amazon is being destroyed, the polar ice caps are melting, polar bears are starving, and Australia is being consumed by wildfires. koala bears and kangaroos are literally going up in smoke, as are many other species, some of whom will now become extinct. These kinds of horrific catastrophes are the direct repercussions of our continual abuses of nature and the environment. The earth and all its creatures including ourselves cannot survive the never-ending patriarchal practice of divide and conquer. By its very definition patriarchy is an unjust and unequitable system. And as long as we work within that system, we are doomed to its toxic effects. We should not be afraid to destroy that which has been so destructive. In stepping outside of the patriarchal platform of the artificially created logos into the lap of the Great-Mother, we can embrace an ethically organic approach, one that is not based on social constructs and patriarchy's dictums but rooted in life-affirming wholeness. Throwing off the yoke of our oppression will take the courage to change the way we live and embrace the totality of all life.

A living justice based on a biophilic ethic is comprehensive, holistic, compassionate, and, yes, fierce. As in the Orphic image of the Goddess Justice swinging the sword of discrimination, we too must decide: Does this support life or destroy it? Yes or no? Ethical and social practices can be created based on the principles of the Goddess that take all of life into account, from the microcosm to the macrocosm. Justice it not merely a human construct or concern, it is the way of Nature. Humans are part of a greater whole. We must realize that Mother Nature is thus beyond our control. And we should learn to cooperate with Her. Indeed, as we have seen from the Goddess myth, Justice is the force/sway of the universe itself, imbedded in and throughout nature. Justice holds being fast.

The first step in moving from ancient goddess myths to a living ethos is the recognition of the relationship of part to whole, where cooperation of part with a greater whole is the solution. A biophilic ethic must be based on the first principle of justice: interconnection. Even a cursory glance of the activism and scholarship around the globe indicates that this first step is being taken through feminist grassroots movements, women's global protests, social and political activism, and academic channels. What is taking much too long, however, is a helpful response from international, legal, and corporate communities that strive to uphold the old ways of patriarchy. Without a doubt, patriarchal institutions both national and international, cannot contribute to this process of forging a new ethical paradigm because their values and structures make them inimical to the principles of interconnection, sustainability, and social justice. Luckily, the totemic quality of myth allows for and, especially, encourages transformation. Slowly, an epistemological shift is happening, and the momentum of the feminist and ecofeminist movement reflects those transformations of consciousness which are occurring on a worldwide scale. The myth of the Goddess reminds us that She/we are an embodiment of interconnection so that as participants, we are part of that living web from which we can neither stand apart nor be divided from. Bound by Justice we are all inextricably intertwined in the intimacy of life. The universe is biophilic and its immediacy is an ethical and energetic fact.

NOTES

1. Mary Daly, *GynEcology* (Boston: Beacon Press, 1978), 29.
2. Ibid., 28.
3. Robert Graves, *The Greek Myths*, Vol. 1 (New York: Penguin Books, 1960), 16.
4. Jane Harrison, *Prolegomena to the Study of Greek Religion* (Cambridge, England: The University Press, 1908), Chapter 5.
5. Judith Butler, *Antigone's Claim* (New York: Columbia University Press, 1983).
6. Mircea Eliade, *Myths, Dreams and Mysteries*, trans. Philip Mairet (New York: Harper Torchbooks, 1960), 16.
7. Mircea Eliade, *The Two and the One*, trans. J. M. Cohen (New York: Harper and Row, 1962), 122.
8. Robert Graves, *The White Goddess* (New York: Farrar, Straus and Giroux, 1948), 465.
9. Ibid., 476: "What ails Christianity today is that it is not a religion squarely based on a single myth; it is a complex of juridical decisions made under political pressure in an ancient law-suit about religious rights between adherents of the

Mother-goddess who was once supreme in the west, and those of the usurping Father-god."

10. Ibid., 258.

11. Mary Daly, *Beyond God the Father* (Boston: Beacon Press, 1973), 69.

12. StarHawk, *Spiral Dance* (New York: HarperSanFrancisco, 1997), 199–201. "A deep and profound change is needed. . . . Somehow, we must win clear of the roles we have been taught, of strictures of the mind and self that are learned before speech and are buried so deep that they cannot be seen. Today women are creating new myths, singing a new liturgy, painting our own icons, and drawing strength from the new-old symbols of the Goddess, . . . The Goddess is ourselves *and* the world—to link with her is to engage actively with the world and all its problems.

13. Daly, *Gyn/Ecology*, 13–14. In referring to the Goddess of Wisdom, Metis, as "the original parthenogenetic mother of Athena" until she was reborn from the head of Zeus, Daly states: "Radical feminist metaethics means moving past this puppet of papa, discovering the immortal Metis. It also means dis-covering the parthenogenetic daughter, the original Athena whose loyalist is to her own kind, whose science/wisdom is of womankind."

Chapter 5

Elemental Justice and the Eco-revolution

This chapter begins the construction of the principles of a biophilic ethic and, in so doing, addresses the question of moral choice. A biophilic ethic is based on the interconnection of all life energy and our codependency with nature. It is nondualistic, nonhierarchical, and certainly nonpatriarchal. Releasing ourselves from false dichotomies places in us a sphere of a living oneness with the universe. This perspective that views us as being interconnected with each other and to the earth reinforces the concept of moral obligation to everything that is. A biophilic ethic seeks to maintain harmony and balance through political, spiritual, and moral principles and practices that provide a comprehensive foundation for integrating wisdom and action in our daily life and in our international policies and communities.

The promotion of global, economic, and ecological sustainability will eventually require a revolution. War is not the only kind of revolution. Revolutions are circles, spirals, orbits, turnings, and returnings, the path of the spheres, celestial bodies, the rotations of the earth, the sun, and the moon. Revolutions are cyclical and not linear, and a new cycle is coming. Recently, thanks in large part to a younger generation of activists, we have seen a surge of demonstrations regarding climate change. A call has gone out that it is time we help heal our planet. While climate change deniers may find it easy to dismiss the scientific data, harsh realities are upon us. We are interconnected with all living beings, and we are dependent upon the life and health of our living planet. While the earth and its inhabitants are capable of adaption, mainstream patriarchal societies are down-playing critical discourse about the issue of sustainability in spite of the irrevocable loss and destruction of so much of our planet's resources. Environmental activists and ecofeminists share a critique of the dominant culture and colonization practices. In the words of Rosemary Radford Ruether: "The key notes of interrelationship, interdependency and mutuality echo across all these perspectives, calling for a renewed perspective of how humans should treat one another and with the natural world."[1] The ecorevolution verging on us is about a new partnership with the earth and nature itself. It calls for a new world order based on sustainability. But, in facing the global and complex problems of interlocking systems of domination and oppression, where and how do we begin to wrench the earth out of the death grip of patriarchy? We can speed up the process of restoration and remediation if we consider the reflective and reciprocal role of our interconnection with nature and the earth itself.

As Malcom X reminds us, "revolution is always based on land."[2] Land is our oldest form of currency, and it is the oldest reason for which one needs currency. Yet, land is not just a commodity. Land is our ground, the earth itself. Beyond it, apprised as someone's territory, land represents roots and growth. Land is the source of food, water, home, and survival. Lands is life, and it is worthy of our protection. Unfortunately, the never-ending commercialization and unequal distribution of land and its resources have created a global food-supply problem, as well as economic inequality and abuse of resources due to lack of biodiversity. In attempting to restructure agriculture, global corporations have turned farming into an agri-business that strips indigenous local communities from fair access to land and its produce. Hiding behind the mask of economic growth and increased food-supply, corporations, and developers are seizing our land. As Vandana Shiva says in the opening of her book, *Stolen Harvest*, "this is really a theft from nature and people . . . but in agriculture as much as in forestry, the growth illusion hides theft from nature and the poor, masking the creation of scarcity as growth."[3] In spite of agrarian reform projects and movements for the redistribution of land occurring in Latin America and India, for example, the effects of colonization on the environment and on the people have increased inequalities worldwide.[4] By denying indigenous peoples and women access to land, they are denying ownership rights, increasing poverty, and preventing us from benefiting from the fruits of labor. Seen in the context of sustainability, not only are people suffering from an unequal distribution of resources but also in a larger paradigm people have become alienated from the land, effectively eliminating our recognition of our interconnectedness with nature.

Imbedded and deeply rooted within sexist societal customs, traditions, and attitudes, women, in particular, are frequently prevented from equal access to land and its associated status. They are denied the benefits of being recognized as producers. According to the Food and Agricultural Administration, women own less than 10 percent of the world's land.[5] Worldwide, women and children are disproportionately affected by hunger and poverty. If women had equal access to land ownership, they would have a reliable source for food and water, and they would be able to provide homes for their families.

The oppression and inequality regarding women and ownership of land can be linked to man's oppression of nature. Mythically and historically speaking, women were the first farmers and cultivators of food. They worked with the earth, planted the seeds, harvested the crop, and fed the community until the role of the hunter became dominant and women's roles as producers became regulated by men. The commercialization of land has destroyed women's economic viability and ruptured the sacred connection of woman and land. Encouraging women's ownership and rights to land, along with strengthening and reenvisioning our relationships with the earth, is a pragmatic, double-pronged step toward changing destructive thinking patterns about women and our planet. Increasing women's access and title tenure to land is a solution toward empowering women, adjusting ideologies, and promoting global and ecological sustainability.

Land as a social justice issue underscores the unequal distribution of power and resources. Therefore, any restorative system of justice must include a return to land and a returning of land to women. This restoration cannot and will not happen under our present social justice system, which is inherently imperialistic. The acknowledgment and appreciation for the sacredness of nature and our interconnections woven into the Goddess myths of the ancients were foundational to their ethical perspectives, and these ancient views contest our postmodern model of industrialized and technological progress based on the accumulation of goods, wealth, and power. The mythical roots of Goddess traditions preserved only a glimpse of what has been degraded in our modernization process of paternalism, segregation, and compartmentalization, with the parallel of the codification of patriarchal law, social norms, and ethics. Today, on an international level, covenants, conventions, and treaties have been formed addressing and articulating concerns for human rights, animal rights, gender inequality, and the preservation of our ecological environment, but participation is elective and enforcement is weak. At least there is some regard to economic, cultural, and social rights and justice issues. Because of this regard, it is often said that "international law ought to be classified as a branch of ethics."[6] But even then, issues and realities concerning human rights, social justice, and ecological sustainability remain stilted and controlled by patriarchal systems of ethics and models of justice.[7]

Seen from the current normative model, inequalities, and desecrations of land and the environment as social justice issues have but one remedy: distributive justice.[8] By incorporating environmental issues, civil rights issues, conflict resolution, and economic inequality, distributive justices seeks to alleviate the "disproportionate harm" caused by unequal economic, race, class, and cultural factors.[9] While principles of distributive justice attempt to operate as an equitable moderate alternative, they continue to utilize imperialistic assumptions. Based on the principles of equal distribution of resources, it employs a value-laden benefit analysis, delegating resources and determining value from preconceived standards. The overarching concern lies in the failure of distributive justice principles to consider nonmaterial goods and those benefits that are not distributable.[10] This results in the perpetuation of domination and nonorganic thinking in standard ethical models.

Karen Warren proposes a new model for distributive justice that includes nondistributive goods and offers a model for what she calls "inclusive justice." Consisting of six key determinants, her conditions are the recognition of nondistributive issues of justice, of justice as situational, of equity as sameness, of the need for the elimination of institutional domination and oppression, of the need for the role of care, and seeing human and nonhuman beings as being-in-relation.[11] Warren concludes by stating that "a main contribution of eco-feminist philosophy is to show why non-distributive issues are important issues of environmental and social justice."[12]

As Warren claims, social justice issues that are based on the principle of nondistribution stress a humanistic alternative and resolution through an understanding of the interconnection between individual and community. To be sure, such advances have gained recognition and popularity in courts of law and academic communities.[13] However, I would argue that reformation is not transformation. More importantly, social justice issues are still viewed within the context of the patriarchal paradigm of normative ethics and ethical theory. Further, one has to ask: How does working from within the very paternalistic framework that created and controls the present situation help women and nature?[14] Patriarchy is its own monoculture, so relief from that oppression will not come about from that self-same system, which treats women and nature as if they were goods or commodities whose value is objectified. Speaking of remediation and freedom from oppression and exploitation necessarily demands moving beyond the system of domination because power, land, and resources have been historically controlled by men as mere objects of consumption and exploitation. A simple re-arranging or fixing of ethical principles and international policies will not be sufficient when the ground on which they are based is corrupt and the bottom is dropping out. Most importantly, however, there is no ethical or moral ground for the necessity of patriarchy. Not wishing to participate in the current ethical discourse requires stepping out of the narrative and envisioning a meta-ethical transformation.

Situating eco-justice within the patriarchal confines of social justice theory simply adds another layer to an already over-crowded and verbose field of ineffective policies, practices, and theories that operate under an elite "top-down" imperialistic model. Because the domination of nature is not different from social domination which contains the current master narrative, the principles of eco-justice must begin from outside the enclosure of patriarchal discourse and theory.[15] Eco-justice has its roots in Native American religion, environmental studies and science, ecology, and feminist theories. allowing for a multiperspectival movement. These various perspectives, both individually and collectively, remind us of the necessity of recognizing the sacred threads and interconnections of all beings, and they warn us against the danger of hubris, in the sense of allowing the part to dominate the whole. eco-justice is essentially biophilic insofar as its motivation is compassionate awareness of the inter-relations of all living beings and our interdependence with Nature. It begins, not with abstract principles, but with relationships existing within a greater living whole interconnecting all life as threads of be-ing.[16]

A biophilic ethic emerging out of the principles of eco-justice takes us back to basics, back to Nature, not as an object of consumption, but as a living matrix of interconnection and life energy. Radford Ruether identifies the common characteristics of this worldview as first and foremost nonfragmented so that the divine is not cut off from the whole or situated in a separate realm but runs "through and under all things." Further, it is nonhierarchical. Radford Ruether describes this matrix as what "both sustains the constant renewal of the natural cycles of life and also empowers us to struggle against the hierarchies of dominance and to create renewed relations of mutual affirmation."[17] The divine is seen as being beyond gender, cultural metaphors and dominant relationships of power, thereby encouraging us to fight against destructive systems and for all life on this planet.[18] A biophilic ethic engages these principles of eco-justice, centering its starting point on the principle of life itself, as a web of energy sustaining, not only planetary life but also that which is beyond the material world as be-ing as such.

Daly aptly gives us a new metapatriarchal take on "being" when she described, it as an intransitive verb, be-ing.[19] Historically, philosophically, and religiously speaking, being has been understood as a noun or a participle designating a noun. It has been reified by cultural, and gender-laden images, fixed and made static by definition and doctrine, and dogmatized by traditions to such an extent that, as Heidegger has said, it is a "philosophically empty word."[20] To put "being" into the realm of the transcendent as an entity, not only betrays its meaning but also misleads us into idolatry. Aristotle, the notable father of metaphysics, referring to his search for the essence of being as "divine science," faced a similar problem when he realized that being may be "spoken of variously," but cannot be predicated.[21] There is no category, which can be assigned to or contain by "being as such." Parmenides, who predated Aristotle, anticipated the rationalistic mistake of over-conceptualizing, and simply stated that being is full of the what is. Prior to Parmenides the natural philosophers found the locus of being in the natural world as the first cause of existence.[22] Beginning with first principles, the natural philosophers characterized life as that which was capable of self-motion, laying the ground-work for Aristotle's efficient causality. In both the *Physics* and the *Metaphysics,* Aristotle equates nature *"physics"* with growth or movement, thus keeping "the verb" in "being."

In calling out "be-ing" as a verb, Daly is putting forth a twofold reminder. First, that words have power in their meaning and that by not acknowledging the verb in "be-ing," we are complicit in "killing of the living, transformative energy of words." Daly warns that, without an understanding of the essential movement of be-ing, we run the risk of simply changing gender names from god to goddess. Thus, the goddess imagery/metaphor is turned into another static noun, when the goddess image itself was meant to represent an energetic process. The metaphor changes everything. Second, and most importantly, be-ing is alive. The habits of patriarchal language and discourse (the master narrative) have co-opted the original sense and sentiment of our most basic and fundamental experiences; to paraphrase Parmenides, that of, "isness." Regulating "being" to a noun, and a supreme one at that, extinguishes the life from the word, and separates us from its living presence. Be-ing as "isness," as movement, as energy emanates from the natural world around us. There is always movement, growth, emergence, change, nothing is fixed and static. The universe is alive. The ancient understood this in their archaic view of the universe as both alive and divine.

The implications of a worldview that sees the universe as interconnected, alive, and divine is slowly challenging our patriarchal notion of justice.[23] For example, the archaic belief of hylozoism, that nature is alive, originates from the gynocentric worldview of the interconnection and sacredness of life, so this belief can provide a unifying perspective for a future worldview of the earth, human rights, and ecological well-being. The early Greek natural philosophers upheld the idea that the nature of the world was indeed a moral order. From nature comes the four (or five) elements, the process of growth, and the harmony of the balance of forces. Along with these general conceptions comes the accentuation of order as justice and as inherent in the nature of universe itself. The significance of this justice brings with it the idea of interconnection, and it is responsible for holding the bounds of elemental and cosmic order. A biophilic understanding of the universe recognizes the dynamic emergence of justice as alive and divine inherent in the natural world, the cosmos, and ourselves.

We are elementally connected and comprised. Fire, Air, Water, and Earth are not abstractions or commodities, they are realities, and they relate to our bodies in very intimate ways, which are deeply (bodily and psychically) connected. We are constituted by air, fire, water, and earth. Air is our breath, and in some ancient traditions (Egyptian, for example) breath is connected to the soul. Air is life force, the *prana* that moves within us and moves us. Fire is our passion, our burning desire, our fuel. Water is both our source for life and that which sustains life. Again, many ancient traditions equated water with life as living liquidity. We are mostly comprised of water, and so, like the tides, are moved and affected by the gravitational pull of heavenly bodies. And we are bone, rooted in the substance of the earth. The earth is our home, our ground, the structure within us and upon which we stand. Many ancient healing arts, including the Ayurvedic system in India and Hippocrates in Greece, see these elementals as working within the body to produce harmony and balance or disease which is seen as an imbalance of the elements. We are not distinct from nature. Our bodies operate under the same elemental laws of be-ing. As Daly states

> for we are rooted, as are animals and trees, winds and seas, in the Earth's sub-stance. Our origins are in her elements. Thus, when true to our Originality, we are Elemental, that is of, relating to, or caused by the great force of nature.[24]

Our existence/be-ing is elemental. In *Pure Lust,* Daly calls for an Elemental feminist philosophy that she intends "to Name a form of philosophical be-ing/thinking that emerges together with metapatriarchal consciousness."[25] By "elemental" Daly means that it is primal, natural and "especially Earthy."[26] Elemental philosophy encompasses both the physical and the spiritual. Going beyond the dualistic divide that sees matter and spirit as separate substances, Elemental Philosophy brings our reason and our passion, and instincts too, to bear. It is original in the sense that it is based on our truest origins: the earth, nature, life, and be-ing. It is earthy and worldly, spiritual and pragmatic. The quest for elemental wisdom is the search for first principles, not a patriarchal abstraction but an actual *arche*, a fundamental beginning. We begin with be-ing, with nature, and the nature of life itself, and this earth, with what is elemental and basic. This approach is reminiscent of the archaic worldview of seeing all of being as alive; this is the beginning of biophilic understand-ing of the universe where all things are interconnected within the sphere of be-ing, As Daly said in describing what she called the first law of ecology: "Everything that IS is connected with everything else that IS."[27] Beginning in "isness" is not esoteric, not speculative metaphysics, but the immediate and unmediated recognition of the experience of life, all life, it is not exclusive.

A biophilic ethic based on elemental knowledge of the universe begins with the basic recognition of energy as life force. Every star, planet, drop of water, and molecule in our bodies and everywhere else is infused with this life energy. It surrounds us and permeates all that is. The energy of human bodies, as well as the energy force in all creatures is a microcosm of the pow-erful energy force of universe. There is no separation between us and every-thing else in the universe. The imagery of the Mother Goddess reminds us of the deep energy connections inherent in the inner workings of the universe and that energy is not separate from the individual person. To understand the nature of this energy is to begin to understand ourselves.

Today, we find the ancient conception of a living universe return to us, not from world religions or ethics, but from quantum physics, which tells us that the universe is a living, vibrating, pulsating interconnected organic whole. Moreover, we are part of that whole as microcosm to macrocosm. Unfortunately, we have been working with an outdated mechanical model of a "particulated" and patriarchal conception of the world where man's laws and social systems have sought to control and confine the universe to fit a hierarchical system of powers and principalities that have subjugated and dominated life. Current laws, social practices, and institutions are antithetical to biophilia, which seeks to reflect the spiritual and material connections of the universe. From a biophilic perspective, the universe is a complex web of living relationships, where entities/life are sustained by and through those relationships.[28] Reality, then, and by extension morality is based on the balance of those relationships within a living oneness, where harmony and order are maintained from within by elemental justice.

As an integrated, interconnected organic whole the universe is inherently just in the sense of balance within the whole. A biophilic ethic is the recognition of this sacred energy connection of part to whole, and it seeks to align itself with Nature to promote planetary life and ecological well-being for the sake of all. As Radford Ruether states:

> the epistemological model we need is not one of dominating mind over passive body, but how to think within nature's own inter-relationships. The economic system that produces true value that maintains life is not one that destroys nature, but one that cooperates with it and fits human life within its cycle of self-maintenance.[29]

And the same is true for our ethical and moral practices, social policies, and belief systems. A biophilic ethic cooperates with Nature's elemental justice, which carries the force of comic order. A biophilic ethic challenges traditional patriarchal ethical theories and practices as androcentric at best, and necrophilic at worst. As was discussed in the first chapter, ancient traditions lived according to the rhythms of nature respecting the inherent order of things where Justice was not blind but a living elemental force of life-affirming energy. The word "cosmos" itself entails order. Normative ethical theories have misread and inflated humans' role within the nature, and have disregarded her superseding order. For us to reconcile ourselves with nature, we need a more robust meta-ethical understanding of the proper order of things. And we need a consciousness-evolution that reflects the principles of life-affirming energy, personally and globally. And for this, we need consciously to cultivate a radically organic sense of justice.

A biophilic ethic centered on elemental justice is not normative or prescriptive, but instead an alignment/attunement of human to Nature and to the All. While trying to avoid the pitfalls of imperialistic tendencies, dogmatic assertions, and patriarchal mutterings, a biophilic ethic has to take as its *arche* the natural tendencies of life. Therefore, the first characteristic of a biophilic ethic is that it is organic in the sense that it is whole, it is one, not two. It is holistic, nondualistic. The idea that the universe is comprised of more than one substance has pitted reality against itself, so that spirit and matter are viewed as separate substances that have some uneasy alliance with each other. In fact, spirit and matter are a part of the same continuum of energy, relations, and vibrations. Think of water and how it can be formed into both a gas and a solid, so too energy takes many forms, matter and spirit. As one of the first principles of ecology tells us, energy cannot be destroyed, but it can be converted. The universe is not a thing, not a substance, but an integrated revolving, evolving, living oneness. Thinking organically allows us to see the pattern (s) of the whole behind/beyond the many manifestations. The multiplicity of phenomena in nature has long lead philosophers and religious seekers on a quest for first principles and causes. Not to mention the most perplexing question: Why is there anything at all? Answer: be-ing. Regardless of what we may think of it (or not), define it, worship it, deny it, etc. be-ing is. In acknowledging existence, we can sense/recognize/intuit the immediacy and unmediated awareness of "is-ness." It is organic. Thinking organically is being mindful of the wholeness of what is and of the 'is-ness" that permeates the all, of seeing the oneness in "is-ness."

The second characteristic of a biophilic ethic is interconnection, as in the relationship of part to whole and of parts to parts within a greater whole, which serves as a reminder to us that everything that is, is affected by everything else that is. Critical thinking and analysis are the bedrock of logical discourse and methodology. By breaking things down and separating them off from the whole, we can find, define and, to some extent quantify the inner workings of things. Dissection is quite informative, but it kills what it dissects and rips apart the living integrity of the whole. In addition to analysis, we need a synthetic approach that incorporates how all things work, both separately AND together within the whole. Nothing works independently from anything else. Every system affects other systems. The ecosystem that we are living in is a vast network of living connections where all parts and whole are interconjoined. One key component of understanding interconnection is causality. Traditionally, causality or the causal process has been viewed as a linear cause-and-effect relationship. But the universe is an interconnected whole and, accordingly causality is not merely linear, but a reciprocally and equally interconnected matrix of causal conditions that are inextricably linked. If the fiber of reality and morality is relationships, then we need a methodology that reflects that matrix.

Third, a biophilic ethic is one that serves sustainability and growth. Presently, many of our current national and international policies and forms of consumption deplete the earth's resources. Working from a "top-down" model, the only thing that seems to be sustained are the power structures of the corporations and conglomerates. Sustainability and natural growth go hand in hand as part of life's processes. We cannot expect nature to keep reproducing abundantly while we cause scarcities and remove the conditions and elements necessary for its continuation. Recently, discussions regarding climate change have suggested that by planting more and more trees we can help the earth rejuvenate. In the United States and elsewhere, people are planting community gardens to help feed themselves and promote sustainability. These are valuable and viable ideas, but they are insufficient, given the economic systems in place. Globalization has proven to be destructive to individual households and families, animals, local communities, and the environment. We can no longer afford having economic growth be our leading indicator. Globalization is not mandatory, and unchecked economic growth has created a poverty of body/mind and spirit destroying communities and natural resources for the sake of "progress." But "progress" to what end or goal, and where does it stop? Many feel alienated and powerless to create lasting change. A biophilic ethic promoting sustainability would encourage a return to community and community-based resources. Working from the grassroots, it would encourage policy changes that enhance our land and natural resources, put power back into the hands of local communities, and protect our environment. Recognizing that we all share the same earth, a biophilic ethic would discourage national interest by going beyond man-made delineations of the globe, and it would replace profit with sustainability as the guiding principle in global politics.

A fourth component of a biophilic ethic is inclusivity and coherence. First, it has to be broad enough to validate a multiplicity of perspectives from different cultures, across gender lines and socioeconomic classes. By validating life as a shared experience, we can appreciate the numerous ways life is supported and nurtured in various societies, thereby giving rise, not to one voice, but to a chorus. In terms of coherence a biophilic ethic can support and allow for the emergence of different types of experiences (physical, mental, and spiritual) without one being in contradiction or seen as irrelevant to another. By validating another's perspective, we are not denying the truth of our own experience, but recognizing that we all see parts of the same whole differently.

Finally, a biophilic ethic must integrate theory and practice, and have pragmatic application. Global markets, international policies and treaties, and social practices worldwide rarely reflect the best of humanity and our highest ideals. To claim that it is time for a transformation of value also demands adjusting our practice and policies to the higher purpose of sustaining life on this planet. This, of course, can only be accomplished through individual and global cooperation. We create change by creating something different.

We begin the creation with a new definition of justice as harmony and balance between part and whole, and of injustice as a disruption of the proper balance and flow of creative energies. In the *Republic,* Plato offers us an insight into the essence of justice that can be helpful (when we leave aside his dualism and tripartite division of the human soul). He argues that justice is our natural state. When all of the aspects/parts of our constitution are balanced, so that one part does not override the whole (e.g., when desire does not override our reason), then all the parts work in cooperation within the whole to form a harmony. Only after we have balanced our inner and outer workings in ourselves can we, then, bring justice to bear in our decisions and actions in the world. Realizing that justice is not confined to human affairs, we can expand our understanding of justice to include elemental and cosmological forces. Nature is not merely the visible order but also includes forces and relationships that operate under cosmic order. The universe is inherently just in maintaining proper relations of part to whole, this is how it sustains all things within itself, in which we participants. As the ancients taught, justice is the sway of being. Broadening our perspective of justice as elemental and cosmological turns on the problem of self-knowledge. Socrates, warned us thousands of years ago that self-knowledge cannot be taught, but we can cultivate conditions for an evolution/revolution of consciousness, by recognizing the necessity of justice in all things. From our thinking to our practices and to our policies, we have to learn to be just with the trees, and all of Nature.

A biophilic ethics recognizes the dynamic emergence of justice as a living dialectic inherent in the cosmos, and it seeks to integrate comprehensive social and political principles and structures that uphold the values of a holistic universe. We are codependent with nature, with each other, and with everything that is, and, in the spirit of cooperation our ways of be-ing need to reflect/mirror that co-dependency in our awareness. This change in awareness cannot be superimposed or legislated. Conscious change can only come about through conscious choice. A biophilic ethic is not based on duty or prescribed notions of good and bad, but instead stands on a single principle: Love of life. Changing our patriarchally prescribed ethical standards from duty to love is not presenting another ethics of care as an alternative to male ethical theories. It is the only alternative for the good of the planet. And it is not a gender issue *per se*. One way or another, we are all going to be forced to change our ways of living in the world. The choice to revolutionize our consciousness is a radical response to integrate ourselves into and within the whole of nature as sustaining life on this planet.

The ancient philosophers (Aristotle, in particular) held that nature has its own *telos* or purpose, growth, and continuation of life. By reorienting ourselves with nature, we align ourselves with the whole. Removing the suffocating voice of the master and replacing it with the voice of nature allows for a renewed purpose and vitality to our existence and infuses us with a desire to participate in and within the unfolding of life's processes. In a renewed veneration for nature, we can embrace and be embraced by energies of life that can condition our conscious evolution.

In all of the above, I have purposefully avoided any direct discussion of spirituality until now. Spirituality goes beyond dogma and world religions, and as such is not easily defined. It relies on a sense of presenc-ing of and participation in be-ing that cannot be contained by doctrine, but can only be experienced, and it in turn informs/transforms our conscious awareness. Spirituality, then, is not only a deeply intimate movement; it is also a political one. Our religious beliefs and faiths have dictated national and international policy, laws, social practices, norms, and morality since the dawning of the civilization. As the personal is the political, so the spiritual is the political. For the atheists and agnostics who do not see the need for a spiritual perspective, that position equally affects their thinking on mores, social practices, and policies. A biophilic ethic requires no leap of faith but instead leaves open the possibility for the expansion of consciousness and spiritual growth. But we need look no further than the natural world. Nature has its own *telos*, its own purpose, and is the very ground of life on this planet. In attuning ourselves to the cycles of nature and the earth, we can learn to view nature as its own "is-ness." Nature is not "thingness." It is a living force. And for a biophilic ethic, it is the main frame.

Many feminists, ecofeminists, and ecologically minded thinkers stand critical of monotheistic world religions and their separation and division of divinity from nature. One need only recall the great god *Pan* who was worshipped in Arcadia for thousands of years until Christianity turned him into the personification of the devil with horns and hoofs. The sub-conscious message clearly indicates that the natural is somehow evil, creating a further rupture with Mother Earth. Seeking to revitalize our relationship with nature, we can adopt a pantheistic or panentheistic view of the universe, neither one of which requires adherence to doctrine or dogmatic faith. Pantheism (coming from the Greek work *pan* meaning all) maintains that divinity is inherent within nature, and that there is a sacredness to existence. Worship of nature is a natural response as gratitude for life itself. Panentheism holds both a transcendent and immanent view of divinity, as that which is both within and beyond the natural world.[30] Pagans hold no quarrel with either of these world views. Without it being a requirement, a spiritual component to a biophilic ethic can be seen as a natural progression along the path to wholeness.

Our ancient ancestors knew the intimate connection between the earth and creative energy. The Goddess myths of descent and return, life, death, and rebirth are biologically and spiritually speaking about the power to manifest life, this is nature itself. In the past centuries, patriarchy has sought to master the universe through control and manipulation of energy: physical, electrical, technological, and nuclear. The challenge of this century is to become more conscious and creative in our thinking and to work with energy in a more respectful and cooperative way by understanding the proper order and balance of things, of the right relationship of part to whole. Not to harness the energy but to liberate it, not by "power over" but by "power within." Seeing the universe as an interconnected flow of creative energy, Daly, on many occasions, called for the "outrageous contagious courage of women," claiming that women's energy "gynergy" was a sufficient condition to create change. Energy is, in fact, contagious and transformative, bringing about beginnnings and endings, evolutions, and revolutions of mind and matter. A biophilic ethic is sympathetic, empathetic, energetic, and contagious. It is all about our thinking, as well as about how we choose to interact in and with the natural world. To step out of the dominant paradigm, a subtle change in consciousness is all it takes.

NOTES

1. Rosemary Radford Ruether, *Integrating Eco-Feminism, Globalization and World Religions* (New York: Roman and Littlefield, 2005), 123.

2. Malcolm X, "The Black Revolution, in Malcolm X Speaks," *Selected Speeches and Statements*, ed. G. Breitman (Atlanta: Pathfinder Press, 1965; 1989).

3. Vandana Shiva, *Stolen Harvest* (Lexington, KY: University of Kentucky Press, 2016), 1.

4. Food and Agriculture Organization of the United Nations, *SD Dimensions*, "*Rural Women's Access to Land in Latin America.*" (June 1, 2001), 2010. http://www.fao.org/sd/2001/PE0601a_en.htm.

Common law dictates are typical roadblocks to women's equality, even in the face of constitutional claims of equality in Africa, India, and Latin America as well as in Muslim nations. Property and contract rights, for instance, do fall within the first generation of human rights; they are civil rights. However, where customary law or religious law trump constitutional guarantees, or are used to interpret constitutional and statutory guarantees, civil equality is meaningless.

5. www.weforum.org › agenda › 2017/01 ›

6. D.J. Harris, *Cases and Materials on International Law*, 5th ed. (London: Sweet and Maxwell, 1985), 2.

7. Radford Ruether, *Integrating Ecofeminism Globalization and World Religions*, 92: "The ruling class inscribes in the systems of law, philosophy, and theology a master class or logic of domination that defines the normative human in terms of this male ruling group."

8. Karen Warren, *Ecofeminist Philosophy* (Lanham, Rowman and Littlefield, 2000), 178: "Social justice as distributive justice has been virtually the only model of social justice to date."

9. Ibid., 178–179.

10. Ibid., 181.

11. Ibid., 187–191.

12. Ibid., 189.

13. This is recognized in the growing trend within university campuses across the United States, whose curriculums have expanded to include programs on World Ethics, Peace, and Justice. Within the court systems in the United States, probation departments have also sought to replace punitive measures with community-based education, awareness, and rehabilitative programs.

14. Radford Ruether, *Integrating Ecofeminism Globalization and World Religions*, 124: "The destructive impact of a pattern of 'dominology' based on top-down epistemology and a concept of the self and its relation to other humans and nature, is widely seen as the root of the evils of sexism, racism and imperialism, with its on-going expressions in neocolonial exploitations of developing societies and their natural resources."

15. Rosemary Radford Reuther, *Gaia and God* (New York: Harper and Collins Publishers, 1992), 3–4: "In short it means that we must speak of eco-justice and not simply of domination of the earth as though that happened unrelated to social domination."

16. Radford Ruether, *Integrating Ecofeminism Globalization and World Religions*, 124: "Visions of humans in interrelation with one another and with nature express this longing for an alternate way of situating people in relation to society and the world. To see nature itself as a living matrix of interconnection provides the cosmological basis for an alternative vision of relationship."

17. Ibid., 124–125.

18. Ibid.

19. Mary Daly, *Beyond God the Father* (Boston: Beacon Press, 1973), xvii: "This book takes on the task of de-reifying 'God,' that is, of changing the conception/perception of the god from 'the supreme being' to Be-ing. The Naming of Be-ing as verb-as intransitive Verb that does not require an 'object'—expresses an Other Way of understanding Ultimate/Intimate reality. The experiences of many feminists continue to confirm the original intuition that Naming Be-ing as a Verb is an essential leap in the cognitive/affective journey beyond patriarchal fixations."

20. Martin Heidegger, *Being and Time*, trans. J. Macquarrie and E. Robinson (New York: Harper and Row, 1962), 35.

21. Aristotle, *The Metaphysics*, trans. Hugh Tredennick (Loeb Classic Library, Cambridge, MA: Harvard University Press, 1980), Book IV I and II 1003a–1003b.

22. The natural philosophers, also referred to as the Milesian monists sought to explain the genesis of the universe in terms of a single cause.

23. Mary Daly, *Pure Lust* (New York: HarperSanFransico, 1984), 260. "For Realizing harmony with the Elemental World implies recognizing the disharmony of the fathers' fabricated world."

24. Ibid., 4.

25. Ibid., 7.

26. Ibid.

27. Ibid., 362.

28. Michio Kaku and Jennifer Thompson, *Beyond Einstein, The Cosmic Quest for the Theory of the Universe* (New York: Anchor Books, 1995).

29. Radford Ruether, *Integrating Eco-feminism Globalization and World Religions*, 107.

30. Ibid., 125. "Rather we need to think of this life-giving matrix as pan-en-theist. Or transcendently immanent. It both sustains the constant renewal of the natural cycles of life and also empowers us to struggle against the hierarchies of dominance and to create renewed relations of mutual affirmation."

Chapter 6

Growing Wheat

What is required for the emergence of a truly biophilic ethic is a subtle shift in consciousness. In order to think globally and ecologically, we need to revolutionize our habits of thinking; however, thinking alone will not get us there. Philosophies, nature-based spiritualities, and world religions have for centuries insisted upon the necessity for ethical and spiritual practices that move us beyond ourselves and connect us with a greater sense of wholeness and energy. This chapter will highlight some of the philosophical principles and ethical/spiritual practices necessary for overcoming limited thinking and for cultivating a global community. Patriarchal ethical theories and practices fail to recognize that the ground on which we stand is a living interconnected web of relations. By daring to step into new orbits of thought, we can spin past oppressive paradigms of dualism and domination and create new relationships and communities that promote and validate life rather than its extinction. Throughout this chapter, special attention will be given to the importance of planting seeds, literally, and symbolically, speaking. If bread is a metaphor for the sustenance of life, then we all need to grow wheat. In this process of sowing seeds, we participate in and with Mother Nature's process of rejuvenation and the Goddess's gift of life, death, and rebirth.

Since the emergence of flora and vegetation, seeds have been the principle source of life and reproduction. The sowing of seeds and their subsequent growth not only represent life but also are essential for food and survival of thousands of life forms. Throughout the world, in culture, after culture, ancient communities worshiped the seed as sacred. Seeds were worshipped before being planted. Harvest festivals were held in honor of the new crops, and people were intimately conjoined with nature and celebrated the abundance of Mother Earth. Many of our ancient calendars and rituals were centered on the planting and harvesting cycle. It should be noted that originally, humans lived measuring the passage of time under the lunar cycle: thirteen full moons, thirteen months, twenty-eight days per month in conjunction with the revolution of the moon. Our ancient ancestors marked the changes of the year in conjunction with the orbits of the sun and moon, with the life cycles of the earth, with the changing of the season and with the harvest itself. In early goddess worshipping and matriarchal societies and in nature-based religions, the year began in dormancy, waiting for spring and for the Great Mother Goddess to awaken the creative energies, so that the earth could be tilled and the seeds planted. The height of the summer was a celebration of life and the growth of the crops, followed by the harvest, and the fruits of the earth. As the year closed, thanks were given to the earth and preparations were made for winter and the Goddess's eternal return. Many of these practices endure today, and their roots can be founded in modern-day celebrations. For centuries, our life cycles have been based on the reproduction and sharing of seeds. Seeds have been our very way of life.

Seeds are the first principle of food, but they are also the repositories of culture and history, of our past, present, and future.[1] Farmers understand the sacredness of seeds, the importance of knowing the land, its biodiversity, its personality, its rhythms, and relations to the seasons, and what grows when, where, and how. For generation after generation, farmers have long exchanged seeds, and with this exchange also came the exchange of knowledge, culture, and techniques.[2] Today, the practice of exchanging seeds has been discouraged by agri-businesses that profit on the exclusive sale and use of "their" seeds. These multicorporations are in the process of controlling the world's food supply, and as we discussed in a previous chapter, destroying lives and the environment in the process. The control of seeds is tantamount to the control of the production and reproduction of food, knowledge, culture, and land. Seeds are the exclusive gift of Mother Earth and her abundance. Turning Mother Earth's bounty into a commodity for male manipulation is yet another scheme of patriarchal conglomerates to control nature and the process of reproduction itself.

Seeds are the beginning of everything. They are the custodians of growth and hold within themselves the movement from potentiality to actuality. Out of the seed springs life, sustenance, and abundance, and it all comes from within. Seeds not only hold the DNA of evolutionary progress. As StarHawk aptly claims, "Seeds are also libraries of genetic information—each seed holds the whole history of evolution."[3] Growth itself is a complex natural process of relations, invisible connections, variables, and conditions working in harmony to produce life. The seed does not grow independently but in mutuality with its environment and conditions and with its own storehouse of knowledge. Seeds not only contain the DNA for their own reproduction but also hold the potential for dominant evolutionary traits and, therefore, are capable of self-mutation/transformation. Is it any wonder then, that we see seeds as containing some form of magic?

It is because of Mother Earth's gift of seeds that life has been able to survive on this planet. Mythically speaking, it was Demeter who gave the gift of agriculture to humans, and not just grain, but the knowledge to cultivate the land for food. Knowledge of the cultivation of the earth, of the land "is of the utmost importance because it is good Mother Earth that sustains life energy and action, it is she who ensures survival of the individual and of the family and clan; in this sense she gives immortality," as Vennucci explains.[4] In Eleusis, during the Mystery celebrations, one of the sacred objects of meditation was a protected grain of wheat. This grain of wheat is symbolic of the sacred process of life, death, and rebirth. This simile of the grain of wheat that dies and is reborn was fully understood through the practice of the Mysteries as a universal process. By providing humans with a tool to overcome the fear of death, Demeter was closely associated with immortality. Demeter taught that existence did not end with death because there was no death, only change from one state of being to another. This is the mystery of life, death, and rebirth.

The sowing of seeds, then, is a sacred task. Yet, as a former urban dweller, as of yet, I have not been able to grow enough tomatoes for a decent size salad. And, I worry, especially in these times, how many of us could survive by growing our own food. Community gardens and "Victory Gardens" are becoming more and more popular and serve a real need for food, as well the sense of returning to the earth for one's sustenance. Growing grain is an intricate process, but it can be accomplished on one's own in a relatively small area. It is an intricate process, though, and it requires planting, weeding, harvesting, thrashing, winnowing, and milling,[5] and then, we still need to grind the wheat and make the bread. All this is quite time-consuming. It is not like "mana from heaven," but it is a gift from the Goddess. The planting of seeds of any kind is a sacred act of creating with intentionality, and in so doing, we participate in and with the Goddess on earth.

In addition to seeds of grain, humans cultivate seeds of thought, seeds of hope, seeds of peace, seeds of derision, seeds of doubt, and metaphorical seeds that can be used and/or abused. All thought-forms, belief systems, ideologies, and conceptual frameworks arise from seeds of thought. Some of our thoughts correspond to empirical reality, some contradict it, some are consistent, and others are inconsistent or opposite. Not all thought-forms are equal, and some modes of thinking should be abandoned altogether. Dualism, the primary tool of patriarchy, is an example of a system that has failed to achieve cohesion and is devoid of purpose apart from its own proliferation. A world order based on a tension of opposites working against each other for dominance is a world order at war with itself, without any internal consistency, empirical coherence, or cohesive purpose. The root reality is that dualism has created a world that is metaphysically schizophrenic, epistemologically divisive, and morally and ecologically bankrupt. By breaking the world order of false opposites, superimposed dichotomies of subjective/objective, self/other, one/ many collapse. We move on, not by replacing one system with another, and not by opposition, but by cooperation within an existing-living organic whole. It is not enough to grow grain to survive. We need to cultivate and explore new ways of knowing based on an inclusive and empirical growing understanding of the interrelations and intricacies of life's energies in all its manifestations. In short, we need to cultivate an organic mindset based on nondual models of thought and energy.

In Western philosophy, nondual thinking is held suspect because it is seen as regulating the world to one being, thereby reducing particulars and promoting universalism. However, nondual thinking is not philosophical monism, and it does not deny the validity of individual identity. Without the limitations of discursive thought and analytical reasoning, nondual thinking moves into radical empiricism, which validates both the existence of manifold world and the reality of our organic identity as part of a greater whole. In Asian philosophy, the world we live in, the world of appearance, *Maya,* is not different from *Brahman.* "*Maya* screening the true divine reality, screening the self . . . and under the display of the universe is somehow that self, that very Absolute, . . . *Maya* is the dynamic aspect of the Absolute."[6] Thus, the world in which we live in both reveals and conceals the energetic manifestation of the wholeness of what is.

In all systems of nondualism, there is no genuine opposition between various forms but rather an awareness of the manifold nature of existence as an interconnected whole. Following Crawford on nondual thinking, the nondual self has an expanded sense of identity and connectivity.[7] The necessity of nondual thinking for the emergence of a biophilic ethic challenges corrupted modes of knowledge and epistemological assumptions based on dualism, and it reflects an integrated consciousness.

There are many examples of ethical, spiritual, and ecological practices that integrate and embody the knowledge of nondual thinking. These practices form the conditions for the seeds of energy and the transformation of consciousness. Think of StarHawk's spiritual and ecological activist work, of communities in Asia and Vietnam which have been nourished and restored by socially engaged Buddhist practices, and of the Native American and other indigenous peoples who have direct and intimate relationship with Mother Earth.

For example, while Native American tribes are significantly diverse in terms of specific languages, places, lifeway rites, communal relationships, and spiritual beliefs practices, they share a common core ideal in the interconnection of all life energy. These cultures are tied together with commonalities in culture/spirituality practices that are the hallmarks of matriarchal societies. For the Native Americans, the mystery of the universe is everywhere. Native American spiritual traditions believe that life and the energy that gives something life is everywhere and in everything. This belief and appreciation for life as it is connected to nature and as the force that connects humanity to the cosmos is the common tie between tribal traditions. Within Native American spiritual traditions, practitioners do not view themselves as separate entities from nature/animals but, rather, as being connected by a common life source/energy that comes from the Great Mother Goddess. This way of life creates a stable, bountiful, and cooperative society of respect and progress. Yet these cultures were subjugated by Indo-European settlers, their traditions were lost to patriarchal dominance, and their voices quieted to a mere whisper. In reviving these living traditions, central to their survival, feminist scholars can find unifying principles and practices that not only can disprove the legitimacy of patriarchal colonialism but also unify humanity back into its prior cooperation with the cosmos and the never-ending energy of the Great Mother.

These are examples of living traditions that ground and yoke our conscious being to the natural world and, then, beyond. In order to cultivate a nondual consciousness, we need to integrate and connect with the Earth. As StarHawk claims:

> If we leave the natural world out of our practices and rituals in any real sense, if we invoke an abstract earth but never have any real dirt under our fingernails, our spiritual, psychic and physical health becomes devitalized and deeply unbalanced.[8]

In contrast to the dogma of world religious traditions, nature-based practices focus on interconnectedness, inclusivity, and the sacredness of the everyday promoting health, well-being, cooperation, and community.

Nature-based practices unite/reunite us with Nature. Since the early dawning of human consciousness, there has never been a point in human history when humans have not practiced some form of spirituality. Nature-based practices place us in the center, calling on the ancient knowledge of magic and ritual. One of the issues regarding nondual thinking, mentioned early in this book, is the concern that it will lead to magical thinking. Historically and practically speaking, however, magic is at the root of all religious and cultural traditions. Humans have been practicing magic for centuries; from earliest myths, magical ceremonies, and prophecies of the sun and moon worshippers of ancient Babylon and Sumer to the Christian doctrines of the virgin birth and transubstantiation. All throughout the ancient world, from India to

Greece and beyond, magic has formed the basis of peoples' radical beliefs in the power, harmony, and interconnectedness of the spirit world. Those beliefs form the basis for modern-day religion and ritual. However, with the advent of world religions, one's personal spiritual experience with Nature became dictated by unnatural dogma and oppressive religious institutions and governments. One need only recall the crusades, the inquisition, or the burning times during the Middle Ages when women were burned or otherwise tortured and put to death for their healing remedies and independent ways of regarding and connecting with nature. Today, in the face of many environmental, social, and global traumas, women and men are seeking ways to reconnect to the ancient teachings; to listen, learn, and incorporate that wisdom. Fortunately, the seeds of ancient knowledge still remain, and, once we reclaim our personal relationship with Nature equality and balance can return.

Our ancient ancestors sought to understand the forces of nature and the phenomena of light and energy. One of humans' earliest concerns was with the process of fertility and the preservation of life. Numerous cave drawings depict early humans' need for ensuring a good hunt and for the continual abundance of the tribe or community. In trying to soothe their fears, early humans sought to control and appease the forces of nature. Much of this was done by trial and error. They worked with the tools they had, the elementals, rocks, crystals, herbs, and the worshipping of deities of the sun and the moon. Work, magic, knowledge, and leisure were all part of the daily rhythm of their life, and all were part of the cycles of nature. As humans, evolved so too did their life styles, from hunting and agriculture and from caves to city-states. As their knowledge advanced, so too did their ideas of spirituality grow into an understanding of the laws of nature, of ritual, and magic arts. These practices slowly gave rise to a more elaborate and intricate body of knowledge from indigenous peoples everywhere.

Magic has its own prehistory and cohesive teachings, which have been preserved in secret goddess cults, initiation rites, and doctrines throughout the centuries.[9] Magic arises out of three ancient disciplines: astrology, healing, and divination all of which were originally considered the feminine arts. The evidence we have attesting to the origin of magic in the mystery cults of the Great Mother Goddess comes to us from within the tradition itself, in terms of secret knowledge, terminology, rituals, symbols, objects of power and, in some cases, texts written on papyri. Magic in its esoteric form is born from the Great Mother Goddess cults of prehistory and literally out of the mouth of Isis. From Egypt to Greece, magic formed the basis of the Eleusinian mysteries. Within the framework of magic, all power initiation and knowledge come directly from the Goddess (or as she has been called, the Goddess of a Thousand Names or the Triple Goddess), representing life, death, and rebirth. The earliest goddess myths were re-enacted as transformative experiences of life and death and between the worlds. The rituals symbolized the journey itself and allowed the practitioner to participate fully in the process of transforming one's energies from one mode of existence to another. The Goddess or the Great Mother is seen as the life-giver. Hers is the power of creation and destruction, resurrection and rebirth. Prior to Christianity, long before the male god, the mystery of creation was the exclusive power of female creativity. The magic of life, death, and rebirth was the domain of the Goddess, and her ways were practiced throughout the worlds.

The word "magic" comes to us from ancient Greece around the fourth century BCE where the root *magus* means wise. Magic has its origin in the prepatriarchal religions of the ancient goddess cults and mystery traditions of Sumer, Persia, Greece, Babylon, India, and Gaul. In the days before the onset of patriarchy, women were the healers, the shamans, the prophetess, and priestesses. In ancient Greece, the pre-Homeric myths of matriarchy and the goddess cults spoke of secret ceremonies, magic and healing spells, and of prophecy and divination rites. Magic is the most natural means for experiencing divinity and realizing the sacred. Magic is highly practical; it involves living in right relation, to one's self, to others, and to Nature. Spiritual transformation, on this plane, depends on concrete embodiment, for without the material world we cannot manifest meaning. The body is alive, and all of life is seen as an expression of the divine, both spiritual and material. Magic is living in harmony with nature. Magic does not transcend, rupture, or violate the laws of nature, but rather seeks to work with the immanent energies and creative forces of the world and life around and within us. Magic works, not by the transgression of laws, but by understanding and respecting the source. It is based on the interconnectedness and sacredness of life and its natural creative process of energy and evolution.

One of the central pillars of magic is that all life is energy. This is an ancient belief shared by the early Greeks called "hylozoism," the claim that all things are alive, imbued with energy of varying frequencies. The Greeks called it *energia*, the Hindus and yogis call it *prana*, life force, or life breath. All things exist through the concrete physical manifestation of energy. All things are pulsating with life, permeated by it. Magic begins with the concrete building blocks of life, the five elements (fire, air earth, water, and scared sun), the four directions (East, South, West, and North), the sun and the moon, the equinoxes, the planets, and the orbits of the stars, and our very own bodies.

A subtle shift in consciousness is all it takes. Magic is about the transformation of energy, and it happens all the time. The performance of magic is based on the intention of creating change. The knowledge and ways of magic utilized in ancient and modern traditions begin and end with the transformation of energy, not just alchemy, with its common meaning of (changing lead into gold), but inner alchemy (changing the obstacles of our existence into the jewels of initiation). Biologically speaking, women perform inner alchemy once a month, or more precisely thirteen times a year. Spiritual practices, meditations, breathing exercises, discipline, and imagination expand the limits of the body to include, not just the physical, but also the physiological, the psychological, the psychic, and eventually the spiritual. The idea that "energy follows thought" is the esoteric principle of all magical rites. The notion that thought can affect matter is transcultural and transhistorical, and essentially about the interconnectedness of all life.

Magic is at the heart of all nature-based spiritual practices. Starhawk, a proponent and practitioner of neo-paganism and modern witchcraft describes the process as a cyclical attunement and a breaking down of the barriers of duality that separate us. In the magic circle, we experience the ebbing and flowing of energy, consciousness and unconsciousness melding together, and we stand as part within a greater whole. Spiritual practices, rituals, and disciplines are the transformative means to radicalize our conscious awareness, from an oppressive duality to an inclusive harmony that allows us to find the path to the primordial source of our being. This is not a mere belief system, but a living tradition carried on by praxis. As we think, so we act, yet the reciprocal is also true; if we change the way we act, we can also change the way we think. As Starhawk states: "To open up to the outer world, we also undergo inner changes and development . . . we need the discipline of magic, of conscious change, in order to hear and understand what the earth is saying to us."[10] Spiritual practices by their very design place us in direct relationship with forces and energies and help us to concretize and manifest a new vision, a new way of being in the world with integrity and wholeness.

Consider the ancient ritual of walking the labyrinth. The word "labyrinth" comes to us from the ancient Greek word *laburinthos*, and the Latin word *labyrinthus* or *labrys* meaning double axe. These roots also form the words "labia" and "labor." One of the most famous labyrinths come to us by way of a myth from ancient Crete (eighth century BCE), where the Minotaur (half man/half bull) inhabited the labyrinth and demanded a sacrifice every nine years. According to legend, it took a hero, a magician, and a woman to defeat him.

Labyrinths differ from mazes in that mazes have many paths, dead ends, and multiple options and strategies. Labyrinths have one path in, and one out, and are about guidance and trust, that is, about learning to follow the path through life's challenges. Labyrinths have a single continuous path to an interior reality that separates the sacred from the profane and brings them together magically again. The spiraling energy in the center of the labyrinth harmonizes and grounds us balancing our interiority and helps us align with the universe in a kinetic sense. Labyrinths are not only for ritual celebration and transformation, but they are also used by women and activist groups, dance and theater groups, hospitals, and prisons as a way to promote healing, balance, harmony, and well-being. The labyrinth is essentially the symbolic portal of life or birth canal connecting us back to our soul. In ancient Sumer, Babylon, and Egypt the labyrinth depicted the descent and rebirth connected with goddess worship. Entering the labyrinth is like entering the birth canal and going back to the womb, when you emerge, you have undergone a spiritual rebirth.

Similarly, other spiritual practices, like Buddhist meditation, although following different methods and procedures, also offer the seeds of transformation. Meditation practices enable the practitioners to acquaint and ground themselves in a heightened awareness. The person who sits to meditate and the person who arises from meditation are not the same; a small, but subtle change has occurred in consciousness that can have lasting effects. Meditation techniques, those that are called "with seed" use imagery to help focus the mind and intention. Mediation practices "without seed," use the breath as point of reference, what the yogis call *pranayama,* to calm and stabilize the awareness. These kinds of practices are found in all traditions and are designed to enhance awareness and heighten consciousness. Asian traditions offer a form of spiritual technique and esoteric principles necessary for the transformation of consciousness than we cannot find in orthodox Western traditions. Nevertheless, the desire to go beyond the normal confines of a binary mode of awareness is as old as humanity itself and is an essential part of our nature; it is the desire to grow, to evolve.

In terms of Buddhist philosophy and practice, we can see that the Buddhist logic of *non-atman,* or (no-self) helps to dispel and blur the boundaries of ego consciousness, thus enabling the practitioner to move beyond dualism onto a more organic awareness. The principle of "interdependent co-arising" informs us that in order for something to exist it must participate in a relationship. The self which exists on a conventional level in such a way that various perceptions seem to reside in a stable abiding entity can be accounted for in Buddhist terms by the interdependent arising of the five aggregates through causal connectivity. The explanation of why there is no-self comes from a level of ultimate reality, even as the everyday self emerges on a conventional level. "Ultimate reality" refers to the five aggregates and the ideas that no-self underlies them, while "conventional reality" refers to linguistic designations, which make it appear as if there is a corresponding reality that actually exists. Instead, these two levels of reality do not exist separately from one another, nor could each exist merely as a conjunction of the individual parts The two levels form a continuum. While some Western philosophers and scholars like Hume can logically explain why the self does not exist, the Buddhists go beyond the theoretical to actually practice staying within the flow of experience. Hence, enlightenment exists, not in opposition to nonenlightenment, but in conjunction with it. This explains why Buddhism continually emphasizes the ever-present Buddha nature as nondual consciousness.

What the Western mind has difficulty grasping is actually what Buddhists practice in being present to the fullness of the moment, not just understanding, but experiencing our interdependence, our fluidity, our connection to what is. This practice has been most beneficial in so many areas in the West in helping to overcome the rigidity and adherence to dualistic and categorical thinking. The Buddhist's teachings have helped the Western mind move beyond the dichotomized thought of being and nonbeing to a more holistic and organic understanding of the self and the world. It is no accident, then, that many disciplines and interdisciplinary movements have started shaping a new paradigm. One possible solution to our confinement has emerged from both feminist perspectives and deep ecology.

One of the more meaningful points that have arisen from a feminist perspective and the analysis of Buddhism has been the emphasis of the idea of the self and interconnection. Given the anti-metaphysical nature of the Buddha's teachings on *non-atman* (no-self) and nonattachment, one does not find the insistence on the supremacy of the self, with its accompanying social schisms of gender inequality and domination. As Anne Klein explains:

> This is partly because epistemology and ontology have become quite separate fields in the West, a rift which has been recently criticized by feminists. Buddhism tends to unite epistemological and ontological concerns in the process of developing categories of subjectivity. The individual is not framed ex nihilo, nor is it dispatched, . . . but merges within a matrix in which it is viable and effective without exaggerated self-sufficiency.[11]

This would seem to suggest that incorporating the Buddhist ideals would provide a basis for eliminating Western notions of supremacy and oppression. Indeed, many feminists have argued that Buddhism, because of its core teachings on independent co-arising with the dynamic between ultimate and relative truth see this understanding of self as a relationship of interconnection as a way of healing and bridging many of the problems associated with our Western understanding of individual autonomy within a social matrix. Feminists maintain that this understanding cuts the debate regarding social constructions and notions of the self. In a truly Buddhist fashion, the notion of interconnection and co-emergence is the "middle way" toward shaping a sense of identity of self in relation to the social world and the world of nature.[12] This understanding plants the seeds for the emergence of a more enhanced ethical and ecological understanding of self as interconnection

The notion of interconnectedness shared by many Western feminists in their analysis of Buddhism focuses on the relation of identity and interdependence of all existence. Ecological interconnections and inter/codependencies similarly form a philosophical foundation for the ecological and ecofeminists movements. The Buddhist notion of interconnection breaks through our Western boundaries, our notions of substantiality and destructive practices, moving us from substantiality to sustainability. Here the Buddhist doctrine of *non-atman*, which denies the distinction between self and non-self, underscores the oneness of the universe and provides us with an ethical principle for sustainability. According to the Buddhist principle of interconnection, diverse individual appearances and phenomena are all related to the unity of existence. All beings, animals, plants, and minerals exist interdependently. Our interconnection with our environment ought to instill in our respect, humility, mindfulness, and compassion. The Buddha taught that our attachment to the notion of a fixed, permanent, substantial self prevents us from attaining spiritual liberation. This attachment illustrates the obstacles in our way to caring for the earth. In Tibetan Buddhism, the "Mother of the Buddhas" is seen as essential emptiness because emptiness is the ground of all possibilities and the basis of all identity as interconnection and interdependence. By breaking out of the bonds of our illusory autonomous self, we can become one with the environment and mindful of our interbeing with all that exists.

Spiritual practices concretize our intentions with embodied actions, rituals, breathing techniques, spells, rites, prayers, chants, etc. All these techniques help to focus and impel consciousness out of the deliriums of dualism into a natural and unmediated awareness, linking our conscious with our unconscious mind. This awareness instills the ethical impetus to practice. Praxis changes us, and because actions and consciousness determine individual choices and social norms, spiritual practices are not merely private personal affairs. Once we realize the interconnectivity and interdependence of all that is, in that very realization, we become ethically bound to all. In these times, especially, we can see the practical and ethical necessity for the evolution of human consciousness if life is to survive on this planet.

This evolution means that we move beyond our normal binary mode of ego consciousness into an expanded awareness of ecological and global identity. This ecological self does not see itself as separate from nature, but instead as being encompassed and constituted by it. The ecological self identifies with nature and acts in harmony with nature's *telos*: the preservation, growth, and sustainability of life. In her work *Spiritually Engaged Knowledge,* Jennifer

Crawford maintains that "this porous ecological identity involves a change of consciousness so that one acts in the interest of a larger ecologically interconnected self."[13] Spiritually engaged knowledge seeks to go beyond the confines of traditional Western epistemology with its subject/object distinctions. It is essentially attentive, nondualistic, and it seeks to transcend dichotomies and contemporary ethical narratives. As Crawford states: "It goes beyond the rational domain to include ethical, affective, and spiritual aspects, both within the interior domain of the subject and in the exterior domain where the other is encountered."[14] This is not discursive thought but instead an awareness. Consciousness is not fragmented from itself by body/mind dualism but is holistically and organically present. When we bring our entire consciousness to bear, we realize, as most Eastern traditions maintain, that consciousness itself is the ground or, as the Buddhist would say, pure emptiness.[15] This consciousness is self-knowledge, in its truest sense, and with this awareness comes the awakening of our primordial unity with all that is. Locating ourselves in the interconnection and interdependence of the oneness means that we are primordially, ethically, and spiritually bound, and we are, in fact, bound. We are bound by day and we are bound by night, bound together in all that is, and the very is-ness as such.

A biophilic ethic reframes both ethics and spirituality as a continuum of knowledge leading into a "spiritually engaged knowledge." A biophilic ethic has its own *telos*: the evolution of life and consciousness. Practicing the principles of a biophilic ethic will eventually help heal life on this planet, but first, it will alter our consciousness. The holistic thinking required for a biophilic ethic opens a new genre of knowledge and pushes the boundaries of human consciousness. As Crawford says, and I agree with her, "what is at stake is an inner direction to which we are accountable and that we must translate as best we can into action in the political domain."[16] A biophilic ethic, then, begins in the middle, in consciousness, as we move inward and outward in an attempt to bridge the divisions that have separated us from nature, ourselves, each other, nonhumans, and life in general.

There is one force that creates, maintains, and destroys: energy. Energy is the life force of all that is. This energy is present in everything; animals, plants, humans, the stars, the galaxies, and even in the sand on the beach that has been made smooth by the tides. This energy is also the ground of human consciousness. Thousands of years ago, this creative energy was identified with the Goddess or the Great Mother. She is not only the one who creates life, but she is also life itself. Since the time of this identification, humans have sought to label and name this energy, which in turn has given rise to world religions and their doctrines. With the onset of Hinduism, Buddhism, Judaism, Christianity, and Islam, women's roles in creation, spirituality, and society became secondary and subordinate to man-made religions. Since the time when matriarchal societies and goddess worship went underground, we have gotten out of touch with this creative energy, which was originally the domain of the Goddess. Generally speaking, acknowledging the ground of existence as creative energy is not a belief system, but instead a way of life; and an experiencing of life's creative purpose. By embracing this energy, we can become better individuals, and the horizon of human consciousness can move beyond dualistic distinction to encompass a spiritual/ethical awakening.

Spiritual practices are the seed of individual and social transformation, allowing us to break out of discursive thought as much as we can within our conventional and social confines. The spiritual horizon that appears before us is an intuitive awareness, a noetic mode of understanding that transcends the tension between the particular and the universal into an unmediated recognition of immediacy, as being encompassed by the world, not as opposed to it. As Crawford argues, this experience is a form of radical empiricism, "which includes the injunctions to love, to wonder, to care, to be at peace—as a noetic injunction," rather than an ethical narrative.[17] Standing beyond ethical narratives, a biophilic ethic rejects, not only the discourse of dualism and normative ethics but also the notion of an autonomous, separated self. As a result, it provides for a more enhanced sense of identity as an ecological self in relation to nature, or as a point of consciousness in the flow of experience of the all. The self is expanded and not reduced, losing neither its conventional and social particularity nor its interconnection to a greater whole. This is the magic of nondualism, and consciousness is the seed.

Ninian Smart refers to the postmodern age as the "era of the unhappy consciousness." The failure of the enlightenment project has led to despair and cynicism. Science and religion also fail to provide adequate models for reality and sustainability. In spite of our overwhelmingly narcissistic society, we do not take our joy seriously. Western models for understanding joy/bliss presuppose the dichotomy of matter and spirit, contributing to the perceived juxtaposition of science and religion. As StarHawk reminds us, "When our sense of the sacred is based not upon dogma but observation and wonder at what is, no contradiction exists."[18] Religious doctrines, and the social and ethical theories based on them, have failed to address the concurrent problems of social justice, ecological destruction, and religious idolatry, and they have, in fact, created them. Asian traditions and nature-based spiritual practices (ancient and modern) do not separate spirituality from science, thereby providing a holistic model of relationships and interconnections culminating in a technology of ecstasy. Such energy models make bliss/joy an energetic fact of existence, as in the Hindu notion of *sat, chit, annanda* (truth, consciousness, bliss). Embracing a nondual perspective expands our consciousness, and our existence, and it places one in the midst of the nature's dance of creative energy.

A biophilic ethic cultivates the seeds of bliss, based on balance, harmony, interconnection, responsibility, and a sense of oneness with nature, culminating in and resonating with a sense of a living presence that is both intimate and ultimate. What the dualistic mind has trouble understanding is that this unmediated state of awareness is not just an understanding of experience, but an experiencing of our interdependence, our fluidity, and connection to what is. Nondual thinking moves us beyond dichotomized thought into an organic and holistic state of awareness and vibrancy of being. We can then attune ourselves and vibrate with the earth, and all that is Be-ing. By planting seeds, we not only participate in the ever-evolving process of life, death, and rebirth, we embody the energy and creativity of the Goddess: we are That.

NOTES

1. Vandana Shiva, *Stolen Harvest* (Kentucky: University of Kentucky Press, 2016), 8.
2. Ibid.
3. StarHawk, *The Earth Path* (New York: HarperOne, 2004), 173.
4. M. Vannucci, "The Origin of the Cult of Demeter: The Story of Hexaploid Wheat," *Annals of the Bhandarkar Oriental Institute*, vol. 79, no. 1 (1998), 85. JSTOR, www.jstor.org/stable41694530.
5. Brian Barth, "How to Grow and Harvest Grains in Your Backyard," in *Modern Farmer*, Modern Farmer Media, modernfarmer.com/2015/08/how-to-grow-and-harvest-grains-in-your-backyard/. One thousand square feet can produce one bushel of wheat which amounts to sixty pounds of grain.
6. Heinrich Zimmer, *Myths and Symbols in Indian Art and Civilization* (New York: Pantheon Book, 1963), 208.
7. Jennifer Crawford, *Spiritually Engaged Knowledge* (Hampshire, England: Ashgate, 2005), 91: "The radical implications of a nondual self . . . reconfigure the entire domain of Western philosophy, challenging the ontological and epistemological assumptions that have provided its foundation. . . . I argue that the non-dual approach, precisely by tackling dualism *per se*, may be just what is needed in the contemporary situation where multiple forms of oppression operate systemically across boundaries of multiple dualism."
8. StarHawk, *Earth Path*, 5.
9. Fritz Graf, *Magic in the Ancient World*, trans. Franklin Philip (Boston: Harvard University Press, 1997), 51.
10. StarHawk, *Earth Path*, 11.
11. Rita Nakashima Brock, Paula Cooey, and Anne Klein, "The Questions that Won't Go Away: A Dialogue About Women in Buddhism and Christianity," in *Journal of Feminist Studies in Religion*, Fall 1990, 95.
12. Donna Giancola, "Buddhist Doctrines of Impermanence and Identity in the Western Mind" in *The International Association of Buddhist Universities: Unifying*

Buddhist Philosophical Perspectives (Thailand: Mahachulongkornrajavidyalaya University Press, Spring, 2012), 215–223.

13. Jennifer Crawford, *Spiritually Engaged Knowledge*, 34.

14. Ibid., 46.

15. Ibid., 58, "I think, a *fata morgana* that arises from the failure of ecofeminist and deep ecologist to acknowledge the ultimate emptiness of (the notion) self . . . my argument hinges on the recognition of a non-dual subjectivity."

16. Ibid., 95.

17. Ibid., 96.

18. StarHawk, *The Earth Path*, 11.

Chapter 7

Thou Art Goddess

This chapter will articulate the principles of Goddess worship as symbolizing the turning of the forces of nature and the embodiment of creative energy. Quintessentially, such embodiment is living justice. A significant sense of connection and responsibility to the earth can be garnered from the prepatriarchal conceptions and principles of Goddess worship, as preserved in ancient myth, and still practiced today. Such awareness not only promotes positive change but also leads to a holistic and ecological approach to personal responsibility and political governance. Utilizing the mythical conceptions of the Goddess as the force of nature, as cosmic order, this chapter is a reminder that Nature is the inventor, and She holds the trump cards over life, death, and sustainable growth.

The goddess is in every woman. Our ancient ancestors knew the intimate connection between the earth and female creative energy. All life comes from women. The mystery of creation comes from deep within, from the womb, from breath to life. The Goddess myth of descent and return, life, death, and rebirth are played out in the life cycles of every woman, in the miraculous bleeding and potential for life that occurs every month and seems to coincide with the moon. Biologically and metaphysically speaking, this is the power to manifest life, this is nature. She is the divine Mother-Goddess, and women, by their very bodies, embody Her and Her creative powers.

"Women bleed all over the world."[1] And there is power in their blood, so much so that menstruation is no longer merely a biologically/psychic event for women on a monthly basis, but has become politicized and used an economical/social tool for patriarchy to continue its control of women's bodies. Over the centuries, women's menstrual blood has become such a taboo that both men and women alike have to come fear it. Many patriarchal religions vilify women when having their periods to such an extent that they are

segregated and labeled "unclean." This is a long-standing tradition that contin-
ues even today. Young girls are taught to be ashamed of their own biological
process and come to see their own blood as disgusting and alienating to themselves. Why is one of the most powerful sources of life seen as "unclean?"

Previously, before men took control of women's bodies, menstrual blood
and women's menstrual cycle were celebratory. Our ancient foremothers,
working and living together, experienced their monthly courses in conjunction with moon and lunar cycles.[2] The womb was recreated in labyrinths,
tombs, and caves, and it was celebrated as the gateway to life. Just as the
Great-Mother Goddess was seen as the body of the universe, women's cycles
were seen as analogous to the life, death, and rebirth process of creation itself.
Further, the process of birth was seen as spiritual rebirth.[3] But this view is
not simply symbolic. In *The Great Cosmic Mother,* authors Sjöö and Mor,
argue that women's menstrual cycles were "the critical evolutionary advance
that initiated human society and culture."[4] Women's wombs and menstrual
cycles are a necessary part of the whole evolutionary process of Nature.
Human females are the only primates to have undergone a hormonal shift,
availing women to have not only reproductive energy but also sexual energy
as distinct from the biological urge to reproduce. With this freeing of energy
came the possibility for advances in human evolution in terms of more mental
energy for social and cultural creations.[5]

Of course, the recognition of the link between women's reproductive
cycles and the reproductive cycles of Nature has been turned and used
against women. As Sjöö and Mor, say: "What was once seen among original
humans, as sacred and magically powerfully to the whole kin-group or tribe,
becomes under male religion impure, filthy, dangerous, negative and evil."[6]
Even many feminists shy away from the idea that women are somehow closer
to Nature, thinking that this is either stereotypical or degrading. In fact, our
ancestors believed in the power and potency of women's menstrual blood,
often using it in rituals and magical ceremonies and even for watering plants.[7]
Fortunately, today's science can attest to the power, the nutrients, and life
source of menstrual blood. Menstrual blood is different than other kinds of
blood because it contains sodium, calcium, phosphate, iron, and chloride—
the building blocks of life.[8] Women's reproductive power is the very flow of
life itself.

Women's periods have come to be called "the curse" by both men and
women in keeping with the idea of women's punishment for the "original
sin" of being born a woman. Today, instead of the life cycles of women living by the moon, we have man-made remedies to control women's reproductive process. Whereas for many women, the advances in birth control and in
hormonal solutions for the elimination of our reproductive cycles are seen as
giving them freedom, this is, in fact, not a panacea but an insidious form of

patriarchal control. First, and not the least troubling, is that the birth control pill establishes an artificial rhythm to women's monthly cycles. Not only are women not in tune with the waxing and waning of the moon, but their internal rhythms have been disrupted and reset, so that there is no natural order to their cycles. An increasing, and most dangerous trend is that pharmaceutical companies are creating products that will make women's reproductive process of menstruation unnecessary and obsolete. Science can now put an end to a woman's period by a mere injection. Are they no longer necessary? The final control of patriarchy over everything that is, including and most especially, women's bodies, will be when patriarchy takes over women's reproductive process. This is not about "birth control." But it is about control.

Man's fixation on woman's fertility is as old as patriarchy itself. This fixation on women's bodies and reproductive process has resulted in the suppression of women's own understanding of creative powers, reducing them to bodily functions, and all but eliminating women's spiritual/intellectual role in religion and the creation of society. Male archaeologists were so fascinated by the early cult goddess statues and figurines, calling them fertility symbols so that their spiritual implications were dismissed and buried.[9] But as we read in *The Great Cosmic Mother:*

> it was women's achievements in the areas of crafts, cultural and intellectual production that made "civilization possible." It was women who were biologically endowed to create human society, language and culture. And that it was men, who were socially endowed by women, who turned around and declared that women were unfit for culture, using women's biological endowment as a justification of our oppression.[10]

Women's labor has been ruled, regulated, exploited, and used for patriarchal profit. While men are worshipping some form of pastoral god, women are busy working on creating. However, women have little or no control over their own production and reproduction. This bridling and usurping of women's creative powers and energies by patriarchy is what has kept humanity from evolving.[11] If we do not evolve beyond man's law and control of society, humans will remain stagnant, destructive, and spiritually anemic.[12]

Freeing women fully to participate in the evolutionary process requires that women take control of their own minds, bodies, and reproductive processes. Feminists, ecofeminists, midwives, and countless women across the globe have long called out on the misogynistic practices of gynecology as abusive and as subverting of female autonomy. Referring to male doctors who specialize in women's health, Daly states that they are perpetrators and that they "are by professional code causes of disease in women, and are hostile to female well-being."[13] Suppressing women's ways of knowing, culturally speaking, was just the beginning of the dwarfing of our humanity, taking over women's knowledge and control over our their minds and bodies, particularly regarding reproduction, is the final goal of patriarchy: For men to have control over what they do not have. Everything from birthing practices and positions, which are more about the comfort and convenience of the doctor, to the perversions of the treating women's hysteria, to unnecessary medical procedures, institutionalization, and the general disrespect of women's experience and knowledge about their own condition has caused women to be alienated from their own bodies. And, of course, all of this is accompanied by the general norm of patriarchy trying to gaslight women, to undermine what they directly and intuitively know.

Today, with the advances in the medical and pharmaceutical industries, increasing women's autonomy and reproductive freedom should be a given, but there is a larger question lurking behind the façade of women's "freedom" under patriarchy: Is giving control of women's reproductive cycle over to pharmaceutical companies, "freedom"? And, in addition, on a more practical level, what role does the natural cycle and reproductive process of periods have in women's overall health? There are now available hormonal therapies, injections, pills, etc., designed to block/alter or otherwise make obsolete women's menstruation. Yes, women are given a choice, sort of, but not really, because the biological fact of giving birth, or not, still falls on women. Perhaps because women have experienced so little of what they need to consider, what constitutes women's autonomy and freedom. In *The Great Cosmic Mother*, wondering whether women themselves may become obsolete if patriarchy gets control over human reproduction, Sjöö and Mor pose the question as follows:

> Do we become "free" by having machines and biotechnology take over all of our physical functions, i.e., is "freedom" a technological state? Or is it an ontological state, achievable only when a biological-spiritual conscious organism is able to experience autonomy of all its functions (rather than substitution of functions)?[14]

This is not merely a consideration for the continuation of the species, but for the well-being of the earth and all its inhabitants. Human nature, society, and culture depend upon the evolutionary process of women—biologically, politically, morally, and spiritually. Balancing the tension between growth and sustainability will not be possible without women owning and asserting their autonomy and radical freedom and by participating in a living justice, based, not on the ways of men but on the ways of Mother Nature.

The myth of the Goddess representing the reproductive cycle as life, death, and rebirth also symbolized the regenerative processes of Nature as life-giving.[15] The Goddess is the spirit of life, and her power is both bio-logical and spiritual, and this power belongs to women alone, as they have brought human life into existence. This is the power that men fear and seek to control, because it is not just about the material world, that is, the physical act of birth—that is only part of the story, it is the magical and sacred power of life, death, *and* rebirth. Our foremothers and ancient ancestors understood women's connection to the cycles of Nature, in tune with the earth and moon, with the whole cycle of creation. Women are/have that energy.[16] This is what patriarchy seeks to control, not just women's bodies and minds but also women's creative energies and not just birth or reproduction but creation and regeneration.

Once a year in the spring, Nature bursts forth with new life from seeds, plants, and trees. Old leaves have fallen away and are replaced with new ones. Perennial flowers bloom once again, and seeds give birth to fruit as the process of life, death, and rebirth revolves. Likewise, once a month, women's bodies regenerate, when the lining of the uterus is shed and, then, replaced anew. Nature as the body of the Great-Mother is replicated in the female body. This rejuvenation of Nature is at the source of the ancients' belief in the Goddess; the idea that life spontaneously regenerates itself. As Marija Gimbutas concludes:

> Thus, the goddess effects regeneration on the universal and individual plane. Just as she effects the transition of an individual from death to rebirth, she also brings about the rebirth of all life.[17]

In culture after culture, the Mother Goddess is the metaphor for this cyclical ever-revolving process of regeneration. Her symbolism (the downward point-ing triangle) and representations (statues and figurines from as early as the Neolithic period) portray more than mere fertility and sexuality, but rather epitomize the whole energetic and cyclical revolutionary process of gestation, growth, life, death, and rebirth.[18]

In celebrating the female form, our ancient ancestors were not only rec-ognizing that when you look to nature, females are the eternal life-givers—from generation to generation, but they also embody the energy of the Great Goddess Herself. The essence of Her true creativity lies, not only in her ability to give and sustain life but also that She can rejuvenate and transform life, even herself and the earth. Because recreation is always happening, both cosmically and microcosmically, the Goddesses' persistent presence, century after century, gives us a connection to the continual primal flow of life at its source, as the overflowing of pure potentiality.

This potentiality is the womb of creation, and although not a new idea, the act of parthenogenesis, seen in the light of the ancient Goddess, takes on a radical twist. The word "parthenogenesis" comes to us from the ancient Greek, *parthenos genesis,* meaning virgin origins.[19] Traditionally understood, this term refers to a natural reproductive process that occurs in some animals and vertebrates where reproduction is self-generated, without fertilization from another. But the archaic mythical notion of parthenogenesis is not about reproduction per se. It is about the ongoing genesis of the universe, and about the creative powers of the Great Mother Goddess as divine "creatrix." Parthenogenesis is possible because the universe is alive. The earth is alive. She is a living being capable of self-motion and self-transformation. In terms of matriarchal thought and Goddess symbolism, the earth is the body of the Great-Mother. She is the living breathing womb of life. Repeat: The creation of the universe was not a one-time event as patriarchal creation myths would have us believe. The creation of the universe is an ongoing process. It is happening all the time, life, death, and rebirth, all from the womb of the Goddess.[20]

Parthenogenesis has been personified through Goddess mythologies in numerous ways and in hundreds of cultures, because without an intimate knowingness/connection of the eternal source for growth, sustainability, and rebirth, we have no inner source for personal responsibility, betterment, and hope. The Triple Goddess is more ancient, enduring, and primal than our current codified, dogmatic, and documented histories. The Triple Goddess as maiden, maid, and crone and life, death, and rebirth, is the recreation of self-insinuating evolution, and the responsible radicalization of each individual's freedom. This may be what Nietzsche was grasping at when he spoke of the "will to power," and dubbed man the creator and destroyer of god. But god has been understood to be male, external, and dictatorial, resulting in a dualistic worldview with a specific beginning, and a perpetually imminent apocalyptic end. Goddesses, on the other hand, have a womb, an actual cavernous womb where life is touched by the spark of creative energy. The internalization of the source of life, death, and rebirth inspires the power to choose to grow, to evolve for better, in the fullness of the present.[21]

In contrast to goddess worship, male monotheistic religions, specifically and especially Christianity, have attempted to pervert the exclusive parthenogenic powers of the goddess. The birth of Christ by a virgin impregnated by the divine father is a shameful attempt at mimicry and is a personification of patriarchy's culture of rape. The idea of an immaculate conception symbolically takes control of women's reproductive powers. Further, to say this was done to Mary without her consent misses the mark. It was not just a violation/rape of a single woman nor of women in general, but an outright attack on the rites of the Goddess.[22] The story of the virgin birth is a deceptive tactic designed to usurp the creative powers of the Goddess and level her role as servitude to the male god. As Daly states:

This, however, is only the beginning of the boggle. . . . The greater deception, the deeper mythic undermining of the Originally Parthenogenetic Goddess required the erasure of her own Self, prior to her role as mother-of-god.[23]

The overshadowing and denial of the religious myths of the ancient goddess traditions give way to the denial of the rites of nature. Thus, the dupe; that men have the power to give life. Not only is this laughable in the face of actual biological facts of reproduction but it is inherently evil in its intent, not just to distract and steal power but also to destroy the Goddess, and replace her with the phallus. The end result, as Daly states: "Patriarchal women cannot create, for they have been made unable to conceive of themselves—of their Selves. Thus, an elemental female tradition within patriarchal structures is inconceivable."[24] And there you have it; there is no place for the Goddess under patriarchy.

The call for a metapatriarchal society has caused men and some patriarchal women to shudder in fear and ignorance as if rejecting a dominant and dysfunctional societal system would destroy the fabric of human culture. Yet, there are other ways of living and be-ing in the world. Matriarchal and matrilineal societies were the original structure for human evolution, and are/were primarily agricultural and organic communities. Matriarchal societies occur naturally in the human, animal, and insect worlds, and in a few women-led societies still exist today.[25] Matriarchal societies are circular communities where everything is interconnected; time and space are not linear or limited by random patriarchal divisions. Matriarchal societies promote equality and cooperation, instead of dominance, community over competition, and sustainability by the sharing of goods and resources throughout the community. Sadly, the idea of shared goods and circulated resources that promote sustainability is not transferable to patriarchal society. In matriarchal societies, women are not the victims of a false narrative that implies that patriarchy is natural and hails aggression and violence as power. The aim of matriarchal societies is, not to have power over "others" or nature but to embody the values of the Great-Mother traditions, to nurture the natural, social, and cultural life based on our mutual interconnection to each other and the earth. Matriarchal societies are celebrated for their functionality, sustainability, and equality, resulting in less violence and conflict, a more flexible family structure, and greater social harmony and sexual freedom.

The close kinship of matriarchal communities made motherhood and the raising of children a whole societal affair. The female body was seen as parthenogenetic, and the role of mothering was revered, culturally supported and spiritually celebrated. The female body in reflecting the powers of the Great Goddess, was equated with the earth, the giving of life and nature itself. Like the oceans and the waters, female bodies were seen as the very living liquidity of life. Spiritually, women were the bond that held the cultural knowledge and integrity of the community, as their role as life-givers is/was an indisputable biological fact. Maternity is never in question, pregnancy is evident, thus, society was naturally matrilineal. The role of men as fathers, on the other hand, was much more ambiguous, and not as revered. But establishing paternity, especially for our ancient ancestors, was not of great importance, and, until modern-times, without the possibility of proof. This situation accounts for the patrilineal obsession with control over reproduction, women's bodies and rights. As Gimbutas states:

> This inability to establish paternity has an effect on social structure because, when the biological father cannot be determined, the mother and her kin automatically are the focus of the family, and the family structure is matrilineal.[26]

Hence, the creation of a patriarchal god to strike down the parthenogenetic powers of the Goddess. In this manner, paternity becomes the law of the land, and women and children are turned into property. The complete control over reproduction, women's sexual freedom, and the overall social structure is the bedrock of patriarchy in contrast with the cooperative spirit, community, and kinship in matriarchal societies.

Still, the living essence of the Goddess is with us and "exists as an archetype in the collective unconscious."[27] In the face of the many environmental, social, and global traumas, women and men are seeking ways to reconnect to the ancient teaching of the Great Goddess, to listen, to learn, and to incorporate the wisdom of nature. The ancient myths of the Great-Mother Goddess tell us how to reconstruct our intimate relationship with the earth. As the source of creative energy, the role of the Great Mother Goddess was also the force of She who turns the wheel of nature. In terms of the ancient mystery traditions, all knowledge and power came from a direct encounter with the Goddess herself. All life comes from women, from the womb, from breath, and from gestation. As pointed out in *The Great Cosmic Mother*, god was female for the first 200,000 years of human life.[28] (For many of us, She still is.) A return to the Great Mother Goddess requires a recognition of Her form as Nature, and as a cosmogenetic unity. As the Mother of all life energy, She surrounds us, permeates us and binds the galaxy together. We cannot escape Her presence (even if we wanted to). There is no place to go. We are part of Her.

Embodying the teaching of the Great-Mother Goddess produces a radical transformation of energy, from a cellular level to the conscious and unconsciousness, on every level of our being. When we think and act in harmony with Nature, we learn to resonate with and within the interconnective whole of reality. The ancient myths of the Goddess teach us that that part of Her function as the force/source of creative energy is to harmonize internal relations with the external world. She is also the avenging force of creation and destruction, good and evil, life and death. This "dark side" of the Great-Mother, is veiled, hidden, and concealed, so as to stress the primordial nature of Her Be-ing, as un-manifested. As soon as we take off our own veils, we can see that this "dark side" of the mother is as fierce proctectress and defender of cosmogenic justice. In addition to encompassing the whole of manifest world, the Great-Mother Goddess contains all possibilities within Herself. She balances the cosmological and ontological forces with a severe and horrific Justice that demands that we reject the dualities of Nature and experience it as a primordial unity. Seeing beyond false dualities, we realize that Justice does not come from without, but from within.

On a cosmological and metaphysical level, Parmenides was one of the first natural philosophers to maintain that justice is not just part of the natural world, but rather is the living force that holds being fast.[29] In fact, for Parmenides, it was the very face of the Goddess Justice who held the keys to the gateway beyond illusion. This living presence of Justice as alive and divine mocks our man-made social justice systems, with its tragic inequality and unbelievable destruction, By affirming the all-encompassing force of Justice and reminding us that Justice is the force of Nature and of be-ing itself. It also affirms that we embody that energy. Even Socrates in Plato's *Republic* argues that as human beings, justice is our natural state. The patriarchal ideal of an objectified and codified system of justice is merely the rationalization for a male-dominated society that bases its entire belief process on inequality and domination. In contrast, Justice as the sway of Nature, although inherently powerful and sometimes destructive, seeks to preserve order, balance, and proper measure throughout. Justice is not about humans per se, and in its ontological sense, it is not a human construct, but instead Justice stands as the guardian of be-ing in its totality.

A return to a living Justice as our natural state requires a reconciliation, not only with ourselves in our own being, minds, and bodies, but also with life, in both its concrete and subtler manifestations. Within the confines of patriarchal structures and pseudo-rational theories and practices, the idea of justice is emptied of its original meaning and becomes antithetical to life. There is no room in man-made justice for biophilia. All patriarchal institutions, practices, corporations, and bureaucracies adamantly refuse to frame their policies in accordance with life-affirming principles, ways, and means. Indeed, some are trying to reform the blatant abuses of oppression, inequality, and environmental destruction. But, under patriarchy, such reform is as, Daly says "potted justice."[30] The fact that we even speak of ecojustice as somehow distinct from social justice, redistributive justice, legal justice, etc. bespeaks the point that the fundamental rupture of justice out of and away from our modes of living has severed us from Nature and the ground of be-ing. The ancient Goddess myths attest that Justice is the order of be-ing and that this order denotes balance and harmony between the cosmos and human moral order. A living justice as biophilia calls us not simply to act, but to be, inhabit, and embody Justice as our primordial awareness of interconnection and sustainability. Thus, it presents us with Justice as cosmic harmony and biophilic balance.

It will take a radical transformation in our individual and collective con-sciousness to bring elemental justice about. In overthrowing patriarchy, the smashing of the suffocating framework of dualism and its divisions begins with the simple recognition of our shared life on this planet as energetically interconnected beings. Patriarchy has, as Daly says: "Broken the flow of our natural connectedness."[31] We have been dulled and diluted by an incessant and overwhelming sense of dread. Change comes from within, by reorient-ing ourselves to new thought-forms, new energy, and a higher vibration. Engaging with and within the dance of life's creative energies propels us out of the mind-numbing doldrums into a basic awareness of the ecstasy of life of that energy that makes our breath go in and out, that pulses through our veins, that makes the wind blow and the tides rises, the grass to grow, and the dog to bark, etc. That energy is everywhere, and the more we rise to the occasion and invoke it, the greater the expanse of our awareness and appreciation for life. Biophilia is a spontaneous and energetic response to this interconnected awareness. Daly and other feminists have spoken of the power of women's energies as "gynergy." Energy is what moves the world. Biophilic energy, like Daly's "outrageous courage" is contagious.[32] Once we find that courage to break out of patriarchy's passionless confines, we can discover the ground beneath our feet. (And perhaps maybe the goddess within.) We will also discover that there is no need to create a new ethic, normative, or otherwise, Justice is already there, in the natural world; Nature never acts without a pur-pose.[33] Be-ing is ecstatic, a participatory dance of matter and energy. This is the energy of the Great-Mother Goddess, it is natural, renewable, sustainable, regenerative, and just. This biophilic energy is also the greatest happiness principle that we have available to us.

Not since Aristotle has the notion of happiness been given the attention it deserves in Western ethical theories. Except for Nietzsche, happiness tends to be viewed as an effect of moral goodness, rather that its cause. Biophilia as a basis for spiritual/ethical attitudes and physical behaviors does not presuppose a theory, but instead starts with the inner experiencing or desire of connectiv-ity with Nature and other species and life-forms.[34] We have an innate, organic, and evolutionary craving to feel interconnected with the natural world, and this connectedness induces happy feelings. This is a natural response to life and all life processes. Biologically rooted, biophilia culminates in a sense of care, shared responsibility and appreciation. Biophilia comes from within, elevating the mind/body spilt, it heals the schisms perpetuated by patriarchy and promotes wholeness and integrity by affirming the love of life. Nature grows in abundance and diversity, giving all manner of beings their place. The primary essence of nature is not only to grow but also to grow among others. All beings, as beings, share an affinity with be-ing, with Nature, and with each other. This is not a mere biological fact among many others. Moving beyond the disciplinary confines of such fields as biology, psychology, design, architecture, and conservationism, biophilia is a conscious state of interconnection. The energy that comes from that awareness both grounds and propels us to sustain that which we love. Biophilic energy binds body and spirit, and binds us to the earth, all its creatures. The source of be-ing that binds us together lies in the body of Great-Mother Goddess. We all share in this mystery of creation.

Patriarchal myths have long dominated our consciousness and unconsciousness with fears of the apocalypse and self-fulfilling prophecies. Matriarchal myths, on the other hand, are about hope and the abundance of life, not the lack thereof. The creative powers and energies of the universe are not just about the giving and sustaining of life but also the ability to rejuvenate and transform life and even the earth itself. In turning into the resonance of this energy, we undergo a rebirth and are revitalized to a higher evolutionary/ revolutionary kinetic source that is both transforming and transformative. Life gives birth to itself. We need a new myth, or rather a re-turning or an awakening to the Goddess. As Sjöö and Mor state at the end of *The Great Cosmic Mother*:

> Women, as designed by evolution as the links between spirit and flesh, are perhaps also designed by the cosmos to lead the human world back, now, to the great celebration of the reconciliation of flesh and spirit. . . . That is, at the end of the world (where we must surely be!) we will return to the Goddess, the Great Mother of All Life.[35]

A dynamic biophilic ethics necessarily accompanies a return to the Goddess, as humanity learns to restore its scared interconnection with Nature and the cyclical ordering of life.

The idea of "Thou art Goddess" is not about yet another mimicry or projection; it is not about looking into the mirror and seeing the face of a goddess reflected back; rather, it is about embodiment, about looking out and seeing the world from the eyes of the Goddess within. Look. Look inward, look outward, breathe, listen, taste, touch, be still, don't be still, dance, I hope you do. In approaching the Goddess, lead with the heart and an open mind. She is everywhere, inside, outside, intimate, immediate, infinite, and alive. She is the ecstatic, regenerative energy of life's unfolding evolution. Parthenogenetically speaking, transformations are happening all the time—from seed to spirit, from breath to life, from inner alchemy to living justice. In the end (or the beginning, as the case may be), sustainability becomes everyone's concern. The earth is alive. We can choose to participate in that process of life and creation, or we can be agents of our own destruction. But either way, Nature will endure, because the Goddess as "regeneratrix" sustains all in Her primordial nature. If you pay attention, you can hear the universe's call to return home.

As previously mentioned, in the ancient Greek myth, when Baubo reveals herself to Demeter, it is a reminder for Demeter to reclaim her parthenogenetic powers. Likewise, women everywhere are reading the signs, embracing a call to a new way of be-ing, and awakening to their own creative fluidity and energies. By woman made, by woman changed so, go ahead, become your own goddess!

(The following is meant as inspirational. It is from my own personal book of shadows, entitled *In the Eyes of the Goddess*. I conjured and created it as a ritual book with my own spells and magical rites, but it also functions for me as a guide to earth-based practices and interpretations of ancient Goddess worship. Utilizing Goddess myth to frame the horizon of consciousness helps me to activate and re-envision my own spiritual journey and return to the Goddess.)

Ode to Gaia

Fire! You are not alone. . .
Intelligence and Passion Dance within you
Fed by Earth and Air,
Tempered by Water
Transformer of Life's energies,
Fast and slow, You awaken Desire,
Spark of Cosmic Fire!

Air, you Tickle me
You make me happy
Invisible and Powerful
You cover the World
The source of the Universe's great Delight
Matter and Spirit, Energy and Fecundity
Word from breath and breath from Life!

Water, Water, everywhere
Flowing free, flowing deep
You are undulation
Strong and sweet
Never to be held under control
You make all things grow . . .
Giver of Life, . . Weeper of Tears!

Earth, at home amongst the Stars and Galaxies
You are already in Heaven!
The bosom of Gaia, ground beneath our feet,
The lap of the great Mother
 Sister, brother, friend, and lover!
Take care, for where else would we Be?
Remain faithful to the Earth!
         dg

NOTES

1. Vicki Nobel, address at Association for the Study of Women and Mythology Conference, Santa Ana Pueblo, NM. March 2020.

2. Inga Muscio, *Cunt, Declaration of Independence* (Seattle, Washington: Seal Press, 1998), 35. "Those not detached from their menstrual cycle couldn't help but trip out on how their own blood rhythm also occurred over the span of approximately 28 days. This is how the moon links up with a form of history none of the textbooks can possibly touch upon: a *psychic* history with all women who ever bled on this planet."

3. Monica Moore Sjöö and Barbara Mor, *The Great Cosmic Mother* (New York, NY: Harper Collins Publishers, 1987), 150.

4. Ibid., 187. "This shifting of sexual hormonal action led to an increased alterness of the brain and electrical activity. . . . Patriarchal religions is, in this sense, a primate religion, trying to pull the human female back from her evolutionary advance over other primates.

5. Ibid., 187.

6. Ibid., 185.

7. Olsen, Hanna Brooks. https://medium.com/s/bloody-hell/the-mystical-magical-properties-of-period-blood-9a5b3e4c34ff.

8. Wikipedia.org>wiki>menstruation.

9. Marija Gimbutas, *The Living Goddess* (Berkeley; Los Angeles; London: University of California Press, 2001), 5.

10. Monica Moore Sjöö and Barbara Mor, *The Great Cosmic Mother*, 239.

11. Ibid., 187: "The fact that the human female is freed from the estrus cycle of other primates means that in women sexual energy is distinguishable from, separable

from, fertility. . . . Patriarchal religion is, in this sense a primate religion, rying to pull the human female back from her evolutionary advance over other primates."

12. Monica Moore Sjöö and Barbara Mor, *The Great Cosmic Mother*, 188: "Female sexuality and evolution have been, for 2 or 3 millennia at least—in a lethal deadlock with patriarchal ideological, religious, economic and political. This is because patriarchy, as a system, wants to enforce and maintain male primate power-dominance-control over our species. The rise of patriarchy was an evolutionary step backwards, in this sense."

13. Mary Daly, *Gyn/Ecology* (Boston: Beacon Press 1978, 199), 10.

14. Monica Moore Sjöö and Barbara Mor, *The Great Cosmic Mother*, 380.

15. Marija Gimbutas, *The Living Goddess*, 178.

16. Monica Moore Sjöö and Barbara Mor, *The Great Cosmic Mother*, 189: "The original magic was always woman's and was associated with a change of power, or energy field, at the time of the menstrual period."

17. Marija Gimbutas, *The Living Goddess*, 40.

18. Ibid., 42.

19. Mary Daly, *Pure Lust* (New York, NY: HarperSanFrancisco), 114.

20. Undine Celeste and Donna Giancola, *Her Underground* (Solstice Publishing, 2012), 190–191.

21. Ibid., 191–192.

22. Merlin Stone, *When God Was a Woman* (New York: Dorest Press, 1976), 228. "We may find ourselves wondering to what degree the suppression of women's rites has actually been the suppression of women's rights."

23. Daly, *Pure Lust*, 103.

24. Ibid., 106.

25. Examples of matriarchal societies: bees, elephants, the bonobo primate in the Democratic Republic of the Congo, and the human Mosuo tribe on the border of Tibet in southwest China.

26. Marija Gimbutas, *The Living Goddess*, 112.

27. Jean Shinoda Bolen, *Goddesses in Every Women* (New York: Harper and Row, 1971), 21.

28. Monica Moore Sjöö and Barbara Mor, *The Great Cosmic Mother*.

29. Parmenides, VIII 14.

30. Mary Daly, *Pure Lust*, 221: "The 'justice' of the fathers Foreground is false, elementary, plastic."

31. Ibid., 362.

32. Ibid., 280.

33. Aristotle, Physics?

34. Jennifer Crawford, *Spiritually Engaged Knowledge* (Burlington, VT: Ashgate, 2005), 204. "When considering global issues a circumference for community readily present itself—that of the planet or biosphere—and we are then able to begin, not from philosophical notions, or metanarratives of the common good, nor from narrow anthropocentric notions of human community, but from an inclusive, embodied community extending beyond humanity."

35. Sjöö and Mor, *The Great Cosmic Mother*, 430.

Bibliography

Allione, Tsultrim. *Women of Wisdom*. London: Arkana, 1986.

Barth, Brian. "How to Grow and Harvest Grains in your Backyard." In *Modern Farmer, Modern Farmer Media*. modernfarmer.com/2015/08/how-to-grow-and-harvest-grains-in-your-backyard/.

Bolen, Jean Shinoda. *Goddesses in Every Women*. New York: Harper and Row, 1971.

Brock, Rita Nakashima, Paula Cooey, and Anne Klein. "The Questions that Won't Go Away: A Dialogue About Women in Buddhism and Christianity." *Journal of Feminist Studies in Religion*, Vol. 6, no. 2 (Fall 1990): 87–120.

Burket, Walter. *Greek Religion*. Translated by John Raffan. Cambridge, MA: Harvard University Press, 1989.

Butler, Judith. *Antigone's Claim*. New York: Columbia University Press, 2000.

Celeste, Undine, and Donna Giancola. *Her Underground*. Missouri: Solstice Publishing, 2012.

Chappell, David, ed. *Buddhist Peacework*. Boston: Wisdom Publications, 1999.

Crawford, Jennifer. *Spiritually Engaged Knowledge*. Hampshire, England: Ashgate, 2005.

Cunliffe, Richard. *A Lexicon of Homeric Dialect*. Norman; London: University of Oklahoma Press, 1988.

Dali Lama, The 14th, Herbert Benson, Robert Thurman, Howard Gardner, Daniel Goleman, and participants in The Harvard Mind Science Symposium. *MindScience An East-West Dialogue*. Boston: Wisdom Publications, 1991.

Daly, Mary. *Beyond God the Father*. Boston: Beacon Press, 1985.

———. *Gyn/Ecology*. Boston: Beacon Press, 1978.

———. *Pure Lust*. San Francisco: HarperSanFrancisco, 1984.

———. *Quintessence . . . Realizing the Archaic Future: A Radical Feminist Manifesto*. Boston: Beacon Press, 1998.

De Beauvoir, Simone. *The Second Sex*. New York: Vintage Books, 1974.

Eliade, Mircea. *Myths, Dreams and Mysteries*. Translated by Philip Mairet. New York: Harper Torchbooks, 1960.

————. *The Two and the One*. Translated by J. M. Cohen. New York: Harper and Row, 1962.

Fields, Rick. "The Very Short Sutra on the Meeting of the Buddha and the Goddess." In *Dharma Gaia*, edited by Alan Hunt Badiner, 3–7. Berkeley, CA: Parallax Press, 1990.

Food and Agriculture Organization of the United Nations. "Gender Equity in Agriculture and Rural Development. A Quick Guide to Gender Mainstreaming in FAO's New Strategic Framework," 2009. ftp://ftp.fao.org/docrep/fao/012/i1240e/i1240e00.pdf

Fox, Karen, 155–175 "Leisure, Celebration and Resistance in the Ecofeminist Quilt." In *Ecofeminism*, edited by Karen Warren. Bloomington; Indianapolis: Indiana University Press, 1997.

Fromm, Erich. *The Anatomy of Human Destructiveness*. New York; Chicago; San Francisco: Holt, Rinehart and Winston, 1973.

Giancola, Donna. "Buddhist Doctrines of Impermanence and Identity in the Western Mind." In *The International Association of Buddhist Universities: Unifying Buddhist Philosophical Perspectives*, edited by Khammai Dhammasami. Thailand: Mahachulongkornrajavidyalaya University Press, Spring 2012: 215–223.

————."Justice and the Face of the Great Mother, East and West." In *Proceedings from the 20th World Congress of Philosophy, Paideia: Philosophy Educating Humanity*, 2001.

Gimbutas, Marija. *The Gods and Goddesses of Old Europe*. London: Thames and Hudson, 1974.

————. *The Language of the Goddess*. San Francisco: Harper and Row, 1989.

————. *The Living Goddess*. Berkeley; Los Angeles; London: University of California Press, 2001.

Graf, Fritz. *Magic in the Ancient World*. Translated by Franklin Philip. Boston: Harvard University Press, 1997.

Graves, Robert. *The Greek Myths*, Vol. 1. New York: Penguin Books 1960.

————. *The White Goddess*. New York: Farrar, Straus and Giroux, 1948.

Gross, Rita. *Buddhism After Patriarchy*. New York: State University of New York Press, 1993.

Guthrie, W.K.C. *The Birth of Western Civilization*. New York: McGraw-Hill, 1964.

————. *The Greeks and Their Gods*. Boston: Beacon Press, 1955.

Harris, D.J. *Cases and Materials on International Law*, 5th edition. London: Sweet and Maxwell, 1985.

Harrison, Jane. *Prolegomena to the Study of Greek Religion*. Cambridge, England: The University Press, 1908.

Heidegger, Martin. *An Introduction to Metaphysics*. Translated by Ralph Manheim. New Haven: Yale University Press, 1959.

————. *Early Greek Thinking*. Translated by David Farrell Kell and Frank Capuzzi. San Francisco: Harper and Row Publishers, 1984.

Hiriyana, M. *The Essentials of Indian Philosophy*. London: George Allen and Unwin LTD, 1969.

Irigaray, Luce. *In the Beginning: She Was*. London; New York: Bloomsbury, 2013.

————. *The Sex Which Is Not One.* Ithaca, NY: Cornell University Press, 1985.

Jaeger, Werner. *Paideia: The Ideals of Greek Culture.* Translated by Gilbert Highet. New York: Oxford University Press, 1962.

Jung, Carl Gustav. *Psychology and Religion: West and East.* Translated by R.F.C.P. Hull. New York: Pantheon Books, 1958.

Kaku, Michio and Jennifer Thompson. *Beyond Einstein, The Cosmic Quest for the Theory of the Universe.* New York: Anchor Books, 1995.

Kirk, G.S., G.E. Raven, and M. Schofield. *The Presocratic Philosophers*, 2nd ed.. Cambridge: Cambridge University Press, 1983.

Klein, Anne. *Meeting the Great Bliss Queen.* Boston: Beacon Press, 1995.

Lama, The Dali, Herbert Benson, Robert Thurman, Howard Gardner, Daniel Goldman and participants in the Harvard Mind Science Symposium. *Mind/Science Symposium: An East-West Dialogue.* Boston: Wisdom Publication, 1991.

Lorde, Audrey. "The Master's Tools Will Never Destroy the Master's House." In *This Bridge Called My Back Writings by Radical Women of Color*, edited by Cherrie Moraga and Gloria Anzaldua, 98–101. New York: Kitchen Table Press, 1981.

Malcom X. "The Black Revolution." In *Malcom X Speak, Selected Speeches and Statements*, edited by G. Breitman, 45–57. Atlanta: Pathfinder, 1965, 1989.

Monbiot, George. "Only Rebellion Will Prevent an Ecological Apocalypse." *The Guardian*, Guardian News and Media, 15 April 2019. www.theguardian.com/comme ntisfree/2019/apr/15/rebellion-prevent-ecological-apocalypse-civil-disobedience.

Muktananda. *Play of Consciousness.* New York: Syda Foundation, 1978.

Muscio, Inga. *Cunt, Declaration of Independence.* Seattle, Washington: Seal Press, 1998.

New York Times. www.nytimes.com 1989/08/29>science-evolving-theory-earth.

Olsen, Hanna Brooks. https://medium.com/s/bloody-hell/the-mystical-magical-p roperties-of-period-blood-9a5b3e4c34ff.

Owens, Joseph. *History of Ancient Western Philosophy.* New York: Appleton Century Crofts, 1959.

Plato. *Symposium.* Translated by Benjamin Jowett. Indianapolis: The Library of Liberal Arts, The Bob Merrill Company Inc., 1976.

Radhakrishnan, Sarvepalli and Moore Charels. *A Source Book in Indian Philosophy.* Princeton: Princeton University Press, 1973.

Ruether, Rosemary Radford. *Integrating Ecofeminism Globalization and World Religions.* New York: Roman and Littlefield, 2005.

————. *Gaia and God.* New York: Harper and Collins Publishers, 1992.

————. *Sexism and God Talk.* Boston: Beacon Press, 1983.

Schrodinger, Erwin. *Nature and the Greeks.* Cambridge: Cambridge University Press, 1954.

Shiva, Vandana. *Stolen Harvest.* Lexington, KY: University Press of Kentucky, 2016.

Sjöö, Monica and Barbara Mor. *The Great Cosmic Mother.* New York: Harper Collins Publishers, 1991.

Spretnak, Charlene. "Radical Nonduality in Ecofeminist Philosophy." In *EcoFeminism, Women Culture and Nature*, edited by Karren Warren, 425–436. Bloomington and Indianapolis: Indiana University Press, 1997.

StarHawk. *The Earth Path*. New York: HarperOne, 2004.

———. *The Spiral Dance*. San Francisco: HarperSanFrancisco, 1979.

Stone, Julius. *Human Law and Human Justice*. Stanford: Stanford University Press, 1965.

Stone, Merlin. *When God Was a Woman*. New York: Dorest Press, 1976.

Vannucci, M. "The Origin of the Cult of Demeter: The Story of Hexaploid Wheat." *Annals of the Bhandarkar Oriental Institute*, Vol. 79, no. 1 (1998): 83–114. www.jstor.org/stable41694530.

Warren, Karen J. *Ecofeminist Philosophy: A Western Perspective on What It Is and Why It Matters*. Lanham: Rowman & Littlefield, 2000.

Wilson, Edward O. *Biophilia*. Cambridge, MA; London, England: Harvard University Press, 1984.

World Health Organization. https://www.who.int › News › Fact sheets › Feb. 7, 2018.

Zimmer, Heinrich. *Myths and Symbols in Indian Art and Civilization*. New York: Pantheon Books, 1963.

———. *Philosophies of India*. New York: Meridian Books, 1957.

Index

Anatomy of Human Destructiveness
  (Fromm), 2–3
Anaximander of Miletus, 16
Antigone, 55
Aristotle, 15, 47, 73–74, 80, 110
Aryans, patriarchal culture of, 14, 17, 54
Avalokitesvara, 61
Ayurvedic healing system, 75

Baubo (demi-goddess), 57, 112
Beyond God the Father (Daly), 37n23,
  60, 82n19
biophilia, 6, 73, 85, 98, 111; defining
  and describing, 1–3, 51, 69, 81;
  current conditions as antithetical
  to, 76, 109; five characteristics of
  a biophilic ethic, 77–79; goddess
  tradition as the basis of, 5, 8, 11, 22;
  living justice, calling for, 34, 65–66,
  110; nature as central to, 7, 80; the
  nondual, preference for, 88, 97; the
  universe, biophilic sentience of, 50,
  74, 75
Biophilia (Wilson), 2
bodhisattvas, 61–62
Bon civilization of Tibet, 13
Brahman, 17, 18, 30, 88
Buddhism, 18, 20, 47; on emptiness, 62,
  95, 96; as gendered, 36n16, 36n21;

non-atman (no-self) doctrine, 93–94,
  95; nondualism tradition, 29–30;
  socially-engaged Buddhism, 52n19;
  Tibetan Buddhism, 19, 61–62, 95
Butler, Judith, 28

Cabot, Laurie, 91
Chenoweth, Erica, 41
cosmic justice, 16, 21
Crawford, Jennifer, 114n34; ecological
  self-identification, 95–96; nondual
  approach, 9n14, 44, 88, 98n7; on
  radical empiricism, 97
Creatrix Goddess, 13–14, 54

Daly, Mary, 53, 60, 75, 103, 109;
  be-ing, describing, 73–74; gynergy,
  defining, 43, 81, 110; human
  survival, on women ensuring, 21,
  49–50; Metis, women's discovery
  of, 64, 67n13; necrophilic state
  of the patriarchy, 3, 8n9; the
  Parthenogenetic Goddess, 106–7;
  "spinning out" of patriarchal notions,
  47–48
deep ecology, 39, 94, 99n15
dikē in Greek thought, 15–16, 18, 20,
  22n5
Diotima (teacher), 3–5

About the Author

Donna M. Giancola is an associate professor of philosophy and director of religious studies at Suffolk University in Boston. In addition to *In the Name of the Goddess*, she has coauthored, a philosophy textbook, *World Ethics* and an ecofeminist novel, *Her Underground.* She has written numerous articles on comparative religion and philosophy, feminism and ecofeminism, and has lectured extensively in national and international forums from Boston and Hawaii to Oxford, England, and India, and most recently, Bangkok, Thailand. Currently, she divides her time between teaching Philosophy in Boston and conjuring and writing in St. Augustine Beach, FL. In spite of her sunny disposition and attempts at being inspirational, she has been known to have an irreverent word or two to say. Lately, she has gotten her days and nights confused, insists that there is no path to hell, and that the Earth is already in Heaven. Her Old English sheepdog is strangely happy. Other projects she is crafting include in a Goddess Ritual book, and a new novel.

www.ingramcontent.com/pod-product-compliance
Lightning Source LLC
Chambersburg PA
CBHW031138270326
41929CB00011B/1675